LIBERTY WORTH THE NAME

•ꟼMP•

PRINCETON MONOGRAPHS
IN PHILOSOPHY

·ℙMℙ·

The Princeton Monographs in Philosophy series
offers short historical and systematic studies
on a wide variety of philosophical topics.

Justice Is Conflict by STUART HAMPSHIRE
Self-Deception Unmasked by ALFRED R. MELE
Liberty Worth the Name by GIDEON YAFFE

LIBERTY WORTH THE NAME

LOCKE ON FREE AGENCY

Gideon Yaffe

PRINCETON UNIVERSITY PRESS

PRINCETON AND OXFORD

Copyright © 2000 by Princeton University Press
Published by Princeton University Press, 41 William Street,
Princeton, New Jersey 08540
In the United Kingdom: Princeton University Press,
3 Market Place, Woodstock, Oxfordshire OX20 1SY

Library of Congress Cataloging-in-Publication Data

Yaffe, Gideon, 1971–
Liberty worth the name : Locke on free agency / Gideon Yaffe.
p.   cm.—(Princeton monographs in philosophy)
Includes bibliographical references and index.
ISBN 0-691-04966-1 (alk. paper)—
ISBN 0-691-05706-0 (pbk. : alk. paper)
1. Locke, John, 1632–1704—Contributions in free will
and determinism. 2. Free will and determinism.
I. Title. II. Series.
B1298.F73 Y34 2000
123'.5'092—dc21   00-024826

This book has been composed in Janson Text

The paper used in this publication meets the minimum requirements
of ANSI/NISO Z39.48-1992 (R1997) (*Permanence of Paper*)

www.pup.princeton.edu

Printed in the United States of America

1 3 5 7 9 10 8 6 4 2

1 3 5 7 9 10 8 6 4 2

I imagine everyone will judge it reasonable that
their children *when little* should look upon their
parents as their lords, their absolute governors,
and, as such, stand in awe of them; and that
when they come to riper years, they should look
on them as their best, as their only sure friends,
and, as such, love and reverence them.

—JOHN LOCKE,
Some Thoughts Concerning Education,
section 41.

Contents

___

Acknowledgments

I PARTICULARLY want to thank Michael Bratman and Marleen Rozemond, both of whom have been invaluable, and for very different reasons. Vere Chappell and John Perry have also been very important to the development of this project. In addition, the following people read and commented on drafts of chapters or asked pointed questions in response to my verbal ramblings, or both: Larry Beyer, David Brink, John Carriero, Fred Dretske, Avrom Federman, John Fischer, Harry Frankfurt, Brad Gregory, Paul Guyer, Paul Hoffman, Nicholas Jolley, Patricia Kitcher, Philip Kitcher, Christoph Lehner, Tito Magri, Ed McCann, Al Mele, Elijah Millgram, David Owen, Vance Ricks, Jennifer Rosner, Debra Satz, Tim Schroeder, Alison Simmons, Steve Simon, Robert Sleigh, Houston Smit, Gary Watson, and the participants in a graduate seminar at U.C. San Diego in the spring of 1999. I received valuable comments from various anonymous reviewers and when presenting portions of this material to the philosophy departments at Harvard, MIT, Stanford, U.C. Davis, U.C. Riverside, U.C. San Diego, U. Mass Amherst, USC, and UVA. Stanford and the Mellon Foundation deserve thanks for my fellowship support. Thanks, also, to Ian

Malcolm, Ann Himmelberger-Wald, and all the other very helpful people at Princeton University Press.

But, most of all, I need to thank Sue Chan, my wife, my best friend, and my constant companion. Without her support, this project would never have been completed and I would have ended up more self-obsessed and pedantic than I already am.

LIBERTY WORTH THE NAME

Introduction

IN THE OPENING of his *Essay Concerning Human Understanding*,
John Locke described the philosophical issues surrounding
"*Liberty* and the *Will*" as "Those Subjects having in all Ages
exercised the learned part of the World, with Questions and
Difficulties, that have not a little perplex'd Morality and Divinity, those parts of Knowledge, that Men are most concern'd to
be clear in." ("Epistle to the Reader," p. 11)[1] And, in fact, Locke
was concerned enough to be "clear in" his knowledge of "Morality and Divinity" that he returned repeatedly to consideration of "*Liberty* and the *Will*."

Locke offered his analysis of the concept of freedom and his
conception of human agency in "Of Power," the twenty-first
chapter of the second book of the *Essay*. "Of Power" is the
longest chapter of the book and was revised more drastically
between editions than any other chapter. Locke seems to have
had doubts about his views from the first: he suggested that
the chapter was included in the first edition only as a result of
the urging of some "friends."[2] The second edition brought
many changes to the chapter and a great deal of expansion.
The fifth edition again brought important additions, although
not as many as the second. And each of the intervening editions brought changes of their own. The result is an interpre-

tively daunting text, and probably as a result, recent interpreters have tended to shy away from giving the chapter a thorough treatment.

The primary aim of this book is to remedy this deficiency in the contemporary secondary literature. I believe that Locke's discussion possesses much greater philosophical unity than it is usually credited with possessing. Further, I believe it to be both one of the most thoughtful discussions of free agency offered in the early modern period and a text from which we can learn much that cannot be learned from contemporary discussions of the issue. In short, the circuitous labyrinth of the text is both conquerable and well worth conquering. Locke kept returning to his views on free agency because he had something important to say.

Locke is one of the most historically important predecessors to modern compatibilists: those who believe that freedom is compatible with the basic tenets of a naturalistic worldview, and, particularly, with causal determinism. Locke has been thought to believe, as Hobbes and Hume did, that there is nothing more to freedom than the ability to do what one chooses to do. Or, to put the point slightly differently, the only aspects of ourselves or our environments that take freedom from us are those that prevent our choices from being effective in the production of behavior. According to views of this sort, freedom is undermined only by chains, ropes, locks on doors, and other physical constraints, constraints that prevent choices of certain sorts (choices to move, choices to walk out of a room) from bringing about appropriate action. Such views have been roundly criticized on the grounds that there are also forces that take freedom from us not by preventing us from being able to do as we choose, but, rather, by perniciously influencing what choices we make. Agents who are addicted, indoctrinated, or coerced, for instance, all seem to lack freedom despite the fact that nothing prevents them from doing as they choose; addiction, indoctrination, and coercion take freedom from us by objectionably influencing what we choose to do.

Locke does, in fact, believe that absence of obstacles to the realization of our choices is an aspect of free agency, but he believes that there is more to free agency than just this. He believes that in addition to having the ability to turn her choices into conduct, the free agent also has choices that accord with what is, genuinely, valuable and important; or, if her choices do not resonate with the good as they should, she has the ability to arrange that they do.

Locke's account of this second aspect of full-fledged free agency arises from a particular orientation toward the problem of free agency common in the early modern period, an orientation that can seem alien to us. Most contemporary literature on freedom has been driven by a desire to map the necessary conditions for moral responsibility. This task leads naturally to the thought that freedom consists in some form of self-expression in choice and action. If our actions do not to some degree, at least, depend on and express ourselves, then we seem to lack responsibility for them; such actions are indicative merely of features of our circumstances they are not indicative of any (morally relevant) features of ourselves. If we were to punish an agent who was not the sole source of her conduct, we would be punishing her, in part at least, for aspects of the world that are external to her and that contributed to the production of the action; we would be blaming her for something about her external circumstances to which she may not have contributed. The trick—and no easy trick to perform—is to explain in what ways and to what degrees our actions need to depend on us and express our natures if we are to be morally responsible for them. Is dependency on choice enough? If so, then how are we to capture the appropriate notion of dependency? If not, what more is needed? Do our choices too have to depend on something about ourselves? If so, what? Values, higher order desires, teleological ends? All these are questions aimed at mapping the nature of the sort and degree of dependency of action on the agent that is necessary for moral responsibility.

Given our orientation toward understanding the necessary conditions of moral responsibility, it is quite natural for us to think of freedom as the highest form of self-expression in action. Something like this thought has been more or less taken for granted in the contemporary philosophical literature on free agency. However, there is another possible approach to the free will problem, an approach that was of profound influence on Locke. In this alternative approach, freedom is not thought to be reducible to self-expression; quite the contrary, freedom is thought to consist, in part at least, in a form of self-transcendence. The full-fledged free agent, according to this line of thought, expresses something better or higher than herself in her conduct; she escapes not just the pernicious influences of the external world, she also escapes her own parochial concerns and biases. Often, although not always, such freedom was associated with a form of religious contemplation; it was through religious contemplation that one could come to give oneself over to God, and thereby free oneself from the bondage of the self. It is this idea, this approach to the problem of free agency, that motivates Locke's suggestion that the choices of the full-fledged free agent accord with what is valuable and important.

This alternative orientation to the problem of free agency has strong affinities with a line of thought grounded in Christian theology. In the Christian tradition, freedom is thought to be an attribute of God, and an attribute that human beings, potentially at least, share with God. An investigation of the nature of free agency, then, might be more than an investigation of the necessary conditions of moral responsibility; it might also be an investigation of the nature of the divine and the nature of the role of divine attributes in our own agency. As Locke himself put the point, understanding freedom and agency is central for understanding not just morality, but both "morality *and* divinity" (my italics, "Epistle to the Reader," p. 11). To think of free agency in this way is to think of free agency as exemplative of an ideal of agency; the degree to which we are free agents, on this model, is a consequence of the degree to which we imitate the agency of God.

In starting to think about free agency by thinking about the nature of divine agency, we might be driven, immediately, right back to the equation between freedom and self-expression. After all, we might say, according to Christian theology, God is purely active; his conduct arises out of nothing but himself, and so, if we are to be ideal agents, we must share this feature with God; we must, that is, be the sole source of our conduct. And, to be sure, this is one path that we might follow in trying to understand the nature of ideal agency. But it is not the only possible path. Even if we agree that God is purely active, we might not think that that is the feature of God's agency by virtue of which his agency is ideal. That is, perhaps to be purely active would not be, in and of itself, to improve one's agency at all; perhaps God would be an ideal agent even if he were passive in some respects, even if his conduct were brought about, in part, by something external to himself. If this is so, then we are no closer to understanding ideal agency by noting that God is purely active.

In fact, there is another way of identifying the feature of God's agency by virtue of which God exemplifies an ideal of agency that is also grounded in tenets of Christian theology. This line of thought begins with the idea that sin arises from bondage. The notion of sin as a consequence of bondage has its roots in the notion of temptation. Temptations, particularly bodily temptations, are consequences of our exile from the Garden of Eden. What comes with our exile is the requirement that we must live by the sweat of our brows: our daily activities are driven by the need to satisfy recurring bodily appetites, appetites that demand to be satisfied. If we fail to fight against these appetites, if we fail to temper our appetites, then we fall prey to sin, the sins of gluttony, for instance, or vanity or lust; it is because we are slaves to our bodily appetites that we sometimes act wrongly. Bodily desires, however, are not our only motives; we are also endowed, in various degrees, with charitable motives, with love. When charitable motives are harnessed in order to battle against our bodily appetites, we approach the avoidance of sin; when we are guided wholeheartedly by charity, by the love of others, we have attained grace. But insofar as charitable motives are selfless motives, to be moved by them is to transcend and escape one's own parochial motives and impulses; to be guided by charity, by love, is to transcend oneself; it is to be guided and controlled by something better than oneself. To be moved by charitable motives is to transcend oneself,

since charity often involves sacrifice and, even when circumstances allow for charity without sacrifice, the agent who is
moved by charitable motives is ready to set aside her own desires and impulses for the sake of others; this is part of what it
is to be moved by genuinely charitable motives, motives un-
tainted by self-interest. To transcend oneself by being moved
wholeheartedly by charitable motives is to achieve ideal agency;
to be moved in this way is to be the most free, the most like
God, who is driven inexorably by unquenchable love.[3]

Notice that the notion of ideal agency as involving self-transcendence is directly opposed to an equation between self-expression and freedom. An agent who attains the highest form
of self-expression in action—whose conduct expresses herself
and nothing else—doesn't transcend herself; quite the contrary,
she concretizes herself in her deeds. The agent who achieves
the ideal of agency expressed by the self-transcendent agent
may not have achieved complete self-expression, but there is an
intuitive sense in which she is more free than an agent who has,
for the self-transcendent agent escapes not just the vicissitudes
of the external world, she also escapes herself. She is not a slave
to her own impulses, parochialisms, and peculiarities. Her acts
of will, her choices, are not the choices of an ideal agent because
she is their source—for all that has been said, in fact, she might
not be—but because they come about as God's do, through
forms of valuable motivation, motivation attuned to valuable,
charitable conduct.

Locke's account of the nature of free agency, while not identical to the account of ideal agency just sketched, is profoundly
influenced by it. In particular, Locke does explicitly take the
full-fledged free agent to exemplify an ideal of agency, and he
thinks that we attain this ideal when our choices come about as
God's do, in a way that arises out of and is attuned to what is
genuinely valuable. Part of what is interesting about Locke's
view is that he also thinks that part of what it is to be a full-
fledged free agent is to express oneself in one's conduct in a
particular way. He takes himself, I believe, to identify both the
sense in which the full-fledged free agent expresses herself in
her deeds, and the sense in which she transcends herself.

This book consists of three chapters. Chapter 1 presents the general picture that I take Locke to hold and examines the details of the second aspect of free agency, the sense in which free agency is an ideal of agency involving self-transcendence. Chapter 2 describes the details of the first aspect of free agency, the degree to which freedom consists in self-expressive conduct, conduct uninfluenced by external sources, and grounds that account in Locke's metaphysics of motivation and his general account of power. Chapter 3 explores a number of connections between both aspects of free agency and Locke's view of personal identity.

I have described the approach to understanding free agency through appeal to ideals of agency as closely allied to one particular line of thought based in Christian theology. And, for secular-minded readers, this may seem to be a drawback, for the view I attribute to Locke may seem too intimately tied to Christian sentiments to be of philosophical interest to those who do not share those theological commitments. In fact, although Locke is at least influenced by, and perhaps driven by, theological concerns, his views are philosophically separable from his religious commitments and are of tremendous importance to the modern free will debate. Modern compatibilist positions have been centrally concerned with cases of agents who lack some form of freedom, despite the fact that what they do is dependent on them to some degree. For instance, one of the most widely examined modern views of free agency, namely Harry Frankfurt's, arose out of concern with cases of addiction and compulsive disorders.[4] Addicts seem to lack freedom, yet they do what they do out of choices, choices that are often reached after careful deliberation and planning. Further, it seems that an addict's conduct is not just actually, but counterfactually dependent upon her as well: If she were to have chosen differently than she did, she would not have acted as she acted. Her choices to pursue the drug arise out of her addiction, but her conduct, nonetheless, arises out of, and depends upon, her choices.

Frankfurt, and many modern commentators who sympathize with Frankfurt, have taken the moral of addiction cases to be this: Dependency on choice—even deliberate, planned choice—is not sufficient for capturing the sense in which the conduct of a full-fledged free agent is dependent upon her. That is, they insist that there must be some further, deeper sense in which a full-fledged free agent's conduct is dependent on her; they insist that there must be some form of dependency of conduct on the agent that addicts lack. In fact, Frankfurt went on to offer a solution to the problem he took to be posed by cases of addiction by specifying further senses in which the conduct of a full-fledged free agent is dependent on her: her choice—or, rather, which of her desires serves to play the role of choice—depends upon something else about her, namely, her higher order attitudes, attitudes whose objects are her desires themselves. But, there is another possible moral to be gleaned from cases of addiction. It is possible that such cases do indeed show that dependency on choice is not enough for full-fledged free agency, but that the additional aspect of full-fledged free agency, the aspect that is missing in cases of addiction, is *not* captured by appeal to some further sense in which the conduct of a full-fledged free agent is self-expressive, or arises from her. Perhaps what cases of addiction show is that there is more to full-fledged free agency than any form of dependency of conduct on oneself; there is more to full-fledged free agency than self-expression in action.

In fact, there is reason to believe that this moral, not the moral that Frankfurt took addiction cases to suggest, is the right moral to take from such cases. Frankfurt's own view, as has been widely pointed out in the critical literature of him, fails to account for our intuitions with respect to cases of agents whose higher order attitudes are not themselves dependent upon the agent herself.[5] Notably, victims of indoctrination seem, to many, to be unfree, yet it is at least possible that indoctrination ushers in not just choices, but higher order attitudes bearing the relationship to choices that Frankfurt takes to be definitive of free agency. We could, of course, take the moral of such cases to be just what Frankfurt and his followers took the moral of the addiction cases to be: There is some further way yet in which the conduct of a full-fledged free agent is dependent on her, some form of dependence of conduct on the agent that is missing even from agents who are indoctrinated. But there doesn't seem to be any reason to think that we couldn't construct further counterexamples involving further forms of pernicious manipulation that point to the insufficiency for full-fledged free agency of whatever further forms of dependency of conduct on the agent we take to be missing in cases of indoctrination. It seems more plausible that both indoctrination cases *and* addiction cases (and, incidentally, cases of coercion) point to the very same moral: There is more to freedom than dependency of conduct on oneself; there is more to freedom than being the source of one's actions.

The pressing question is this: What more could there be to free agency than self-expression? And it is in answer to this question that Locke's views are strikingly relevant to the modern free will debate, for it is just this question that Locke aims to answer. Locke aims to answer this question through appeal to an ideal of agency bearing strong affinities to a theological ideal; he appeals to an ideal that we can fall short of achieving even once we are the source of our own conduct in all the ways he takes to be important or possible. But, I believe (although I won't be arguing for the point here) that our intuitions about cases of addiction, indoctrination, and coercion are also driven by a conception of an ideal of agency that we take such agents to fall short of achieving.[6] Locke's ideal of agency is closely related to an ideal based in Christian theology, but our concept of free agency is, I believe, intimately tied up with conceptions of ideal agency also, conceptions that may or may not have their source in Christian ideology, but nonetheless inform our intuitions about freedom. In fact, it is very possible that our ideal of agency is a secularly expressed form of just the same ideal that Locke describes and appeals to. And so it is possible that Locke's view of free agency gives us insight not just into the nature of divinity and the divinity in us, but also into the nature of freedom of the sort that the vehemently secular take us to be capable, on occasion, of achieving.[7]

I

A Second Perfection

LOCKE's central discussion of the nature of freedom and the metaphysics of agency ("Of Power," II.XXI) follows a pattern typical in the *Essay*. Throughout the second book of the *Essay*, Locke attempts to show how we acquire ideas of various sorts through the processes that he allows: simple ideas are acquired through sensation and reflection; these are the building blocks of complex ideas created either voluntarily by the mind, or received in bundles from external objects. However, Locke rarely confines himself to describing the mechanics of the acquisition of the ideas under consideration; rather, he moves fluidly into consideration of a range of philosophical questions concerning those ideas and their objects.

The ostensible purpose of "Of Power" is to explain how it is that we acquire the ideas that we have of the powers of particular objects. Powers are states of objects by virtue of which objects have changes produced in themselves when in certain circumstances (passive powers) or states by virtue of which they produce changes in other objects in certain circumstances (active powers).[1] Locke's empiricism demands a positive account of the mechanism by which we come to have ideas of powers, and such an account might be very difficult to provide: after all, we do not generally observe what it is about objects that accounts for the fact that they engage in directly observable changes or states. Active powers pose a particular problem, for we often have the idea that an object has a particular active power (such as the sun's power to melt wax) without ever observing any change in the object itself; that is, we often observe only changes in other objects. Locke's claim in II.XXI.4 that we get the idea of active powers from reflection on our own ability to produce movement in our bodies or thoughts in our minds (a claim, incidentally, that Hume and Malebranche argue forcefully against[2]) leads him directly to his reflections on the nature of volition and voluntary action: If we receive our ideas of active powers from reflection on our ability to act, what is it that we learn about that power in ourselves when we so reflect? What is that power like? What are its limitations and what is its nature? The remainder of the chapter is an attempt to say what we learn. What emerges by the end of the chapter is a detailed conception of free agency.

Freedom of Action

The definition of freedom (what I will call, for convenience, "freedom of action") that Locke offers is inherited from Hobbes. In "Of Liberty and Necessity," Hobbes says:

> For he is free to do a thing, that may do it if he have the will to do it, and may forbear, if he have the will to forbear. (*English Works* 4:240)[3]

Locke offers various remarks throughout the chapter that sound a great deal like this. For instance:

> [S]o far as a Man has power to think or not to think, to move or not to move, according to the preference or direction of his own mind, so far is a Man *Free*. Where-ever any performance or forbearance are not equally in a Man's power; where-ever doing or not doing will not equally follow upon the preference of his mind directing it, there he is not *Free*. . . . So that the *Idea* of *Liberty* is, the *Idea* of a power in any Agent to do or forbear any particular Action, according to the determination or thought of the mind,

whereby either of them is preferr'd to the other: where either of them is not in the Power of the Agent to be produced by him according to his *Volition*, there he is not at *Liberty*; that Agent is under *Necessity*. (II.XXI.8)

Liberty . . . is the power a Man has to do or forbear doing any particular Action according as its doing or forbearance has the actual preference in the Mind; which is the same thing as to say, according as he himself *wills* it. (II.XXI.15)

[S]o far as any one can, by the direction or choice of his Mind, preferring the existence of any Action, to the non-existence of that Action, and *vice versa*, make it to exist, or not exist, so far he is *free*. (II.XXI.21)

Freedom consists in the dependence of the Existence, or not Existence of any Action, upon our Volition of it. (II.XXI.27)

Liberty, 'tis plain, consists in a Power to do, or not to do; to do, or forbear doing, as we *will*. (II.XXI.56)

For Locke, freedom with respect to a particular action is what an agent has when she has a pair of abilities or powers: she must be able to perform the action voluntarily and she must be able to forbear from the action voluntarily. As a modification of an agent is voluntary by virtue of the fact that it bears some intimate relation to a volition on the agent's part—I call the relation "satisfaction" and discuss it at length in the next chapter—in the above passages, Locke describes the dual ability that the agent must have for freedom of action as a kind of dependence of the occurrence or nonoccurrence of action on the will. It must be "up to the agent" whether she engages in a particular modification or does not if the agent is to have freedom of action with respect to the modification; here, "up to the agent" is analyzed as "determined by the content of the agent's volition."

From the passages just quoted, then, we have a view of freedom of action—an agent has it when she has the ability to act voluntarily and the ability to forbear voluntarily—that raises as many questions as it answers. In particular, we want to know what is true of an agent who has each of these abilities. That is, we want a list of conditions that are satisfied by all and only those agents who have these two abilities. How are we to cash out what it is to have both the ability to act voluntarily and the ability to refrain voluntarily?

For the purposes of this chapter, it is enough to formalize Locke's view of freedom of action as follows:

Freedom of Action: An agent has freedom of action with respect to A *if and only if* (1) if she chooses to A, she will A voluntarily, and (2) there is some other action, B, incompatible with A, such that if she chooses to B, she will B voluntarily.

Clause (1) is intended to capture what, for Locke, it is to have the power to voluntarily act, clause (2), the power to voluntarily refrain. Since the account of freedom of action makes no reference to powers but, rather, reduces the possession of a power to the truth of a particular conditional, the account assumes that, for Locke, it is both necessary and sufficient for the possession of a power to A that a conditional of the form "If the agent (or substance) is in circumstances C, she (or it) engages in a modification of type A" is true of the agent (or substance). I argue for this interpretive claim in chapter 2. In addition, the account of freedom of action remains agnostic about the exact details of Locke's account of voluntary action, and so it is not a full analysis of Locke's account of freedom of action. In chapter 2, I provide an analysis of Locke's account of voluntary action that can be used to fill in the details of this account of freedom of action.

A short digression with regard to clause (2): We might replace clause (2) with (2′) If she wills not to A, then she will voluntarily not-A. The difference between (2) and (2′) is this: (2) assumes that it is sufficient for an agent to voluntarily refrain from A that she voluntarily do something incompatible with A-ing; (2′), on the other hand, assumes that a voluntary refraining only occurs when the actual absence of action is itself voluntary. The two interpretations can come apart. For instance, imagine that my psychology is such that if I choose to put thoughts concerning Agatha Christie out of my mind, such a choice invariably has just the opposite effect; just choosing not to think about Agatha Christie is enough to cause me to think about her. Do I have freedom of action with respect to the action of thinking about Agatha Christie? Well, under (2) I do, for if I simply make a choice to think about, say, Dashiell Hammett, and at the same time don't make a choice not to think about Agatha Christie, I will voluntarily think about Hammett instead. Under (2′), I do not have freedom of action, for if I choose not to think about Christie, I will still think about her. The question is whether, for Locke, I would be voluntarily refraining from thinking about Christie when I voluntarily think about Hammett instead. There are few texts in the *Essay* that directly discuss the conditions for refraining or forbearance from action, and those few passages that are relevant can be plausibly interpreted either way. For instance:

> To avoid multiplying of words, I would crave leave here, under the word *Action*, to comprehend the forbearance too of any Action proposed; *sitting still*, or *holding one's peace*, when *walking* or *speaking* are propos'd, though mere forbearances, requiring as much the determination of the *Will*, and being often as weighty in their consequences, as the contrary Actions, may, on that consideration, well enough pass for Actions too. (II.XXI.28)

Although Locke acknowledges here that "sitting still" or "holding one's peace" require "the determination of the *Will*," he doesn't say what "determination" is required. Does the agent who voluntarily refrains from standing up by voluntarily sitting still choose to sit still (an action incompatible with standing up) or does she choose not to stand up? This passage cannot be used to settle the question, and I do not know of other texts that are any more useful for settling the dispute. But, I consider (2) a more philosophically plausible condition on freedom of action than (2′); after all, an agent who tries to excuse herself from responsibility for acting as she did cannot insist that she could not have done otherwise merely because she would not have done otherwise had she chosen not to, if it is also the case that she would have done otherwise had she chosen, instead, to do something other than what she did. Since (2) is more likely to be true and is, at the very least, compatible with the texts, I will be assuming from here on that it is that view which Locke holds.[4]

Asserting that a being has freedom of action with respect to a particular action is to assert that clauses (1) and (2) of the account of freedom of action are true of the being. But notice that for all that has been said so far, a stone or a tree, or any other object lacking even the potential to engage in an act of will, can be in a circumstance such that *if* it were to engage in a relevant act of will, the relevant results would occur. It follows that for all that has been said so far, beings that are clearly not capable of freedom or unfreedom can possess freedom of action. Locke heads off this worry, however, in the following passage:

> *Liberty* cannot be, where there is no Thought, no Volition, no Will. . . . A Tennis-ball, whether in motion by the stroke of a Racket, or lying still at rest, is not by any one taken to be a *free Agent*. If we enquire into the Reason, we shall find it is, because we conceive not a Tennis-ball to think, and consequently not to have any Volition, or preference of Motion to rest, or *vice versa*; and therefore has not *Liberty*, is not a free Agent. (II.XXI.8–9)

Locke's idea here is that for freedom of action with respect to a particular action, not only do the conditions described in the account need to be satisfied, but an additional condition must be satisfied as well: the being whose freedom is being assessed must be the sort of thing that can make choices, it must be possessed with a will. But notice that it is not required for freedom of action with respect to a particular action that the agent be capable of making a particular choice in favor of either that action or an incompatible alternative, but only that the agent be capable of making choices in general. That is, Locke does not require for freedom of action with respect to a particular action that the agent have the power to *choose* both the action and the alternative action, but only that each action would come about were the agent to so choose, *and* the agent must be the sort of thing that is capable of making choices.

Am I free right now to pick up my computer and smash it against the wall? There is a sense of "free" in which I am. This is so despite the fact that given my attachment to my computer and my generally stingy attitude, I am not capable of choosing to do so; nothing that I can plausibly envision happening right now would override the psychological forces that prevent me from so choosing. This is not to say that we cannot trump up some story in which I would so choose; rather it is to say that my circumstances would have to be radically altered for me to make such a choice. The sense in which I am free to throw my computer across the room despite my inability to choose to do so is what is captured by Locke's notion of freedom of action.

Notice that if an agent has freedom of action, then she has a kind of control over her conduct. Her conduct is responsive to her state; whether she performs a particular action or an action incompatible with it depends on what volition she has. Therefore, when she has freedom of action, what she does is, in some sense at least, "up to her," for something about her—namely, the content of her choice—determines what she does. If she acts voluntarily, her action expresses her volition, and thereby her power to produce volitions, her will. However, an agent's voluntary action needn't express her freedom of action, for she could have acted voluntarily while failing to have freedom of action, for freedom of action is a *dual* power, and the occurrence of a voluntary action expresses only the agent's ability to voluntarily act in the way she acted, not her ability to voluntarily act in a way contrary to it. Locke illustrates this result with cases of overdetermination of action: If a man stays in a room willingly even though the room is locked, then he stays voluntarily even though he is not free with respect to staying: his staying satisfies his volition to stay, but there is no action incompatible with staying such that if he had willed it, he would have done it in the appropriate way. And Locke takes this result—as any compatibilist would—to be welcome: To act voluntarily is to participate in one's action in a particular way.[5] In fact, such participation is necessary for many forms of moral responsibility. So even if it is agreed that some form of causal determinism undermines freedom of action, it would not follow that all forms of moral responsibility are undermined by causal determinism.[6]

Locke's notion of freedom of action is not sufficient for capturing all the senses and sorts of freedom that we are after when we worry about free agency. If, for instance, my volition comes about as a result of, among other things, addiction, phobia, deception, indoctrination, or coercion, then my action will not be free in all the senses that we imagine possible, even though I might very well have had freedom of action with respect to it. But what else are we after?

Let's take it for granted that an agent who has freedom of action in Locke's sense is not, necessarily, a full-fledged free agent in all the senses that we are after, since she might be addicted, or indoctrinated or coerced. Let's call the additional abilities possessed or conditions satisfied by a full-fledged free agent "the Elusive Something." Hobbes can be taken to have rejected the reality of the Elusive Something; he denied that there was anything over and above freedom of action possessed by the full-fledged free agent. Hobbes was roundly criticized for this opinion by, among others, Bishop Bramhall. For instance, in his 1648 correspondence with Hobbes, Bramhall wrote:

> If [a man's] will do not come upon him according to his will, then he is not a free ... agent. ... Certainly all the freedom of the agent is from the freedom of the will. If the will have no power over itself, the agent is no more free than a staff in a man's hand. ... If the action be free to write or to forbear, the power or faculty to will or nill, must of necessity be more free.[7]

Bramhall here expresses both a firm belief that there is an Elusive Something, and a suggestion as to what the Elusive Something is: an agent has the Elusive Something *if and only if* "her will comes upon her according to her will."[8] But there is something else to note about this passage: Bramhall seems to say that an agent who possesses the Elusive Something as he analyzes it has another kind of freedom, a freedom of the will.

In short, Bramhall takes the Elusive Something to be control of the will by the will itself, and he takes that to be freedom of the will. So, there are two propositions to be considered here that are potentially separable: (1) there is an Elusive Something—that is, we need more than freedom of action to be full-fledged free agents, and (2) the Elusive Something is "freedom of will." Hobbes rejects both propositions, Bramhall accepts both. What is Locke's attitude toward these two propositions?

Locke accepts (1). He believes that there are conditions that an agent needs to fulfill in order to be a truly free agent that are not specified in his account of freedom of action. He also believes that an agent who satisfies these conditions does not, literally speaking, have any form of freedom that she would have lacked had she not satisfied these conditions; that is, he rejects (2). However, he also holds—in the second and later editions of the *Essay*—that an agent who has the Elusive Something has something that we mistakenly call "freedom of will"; it is a mistake to call it that, since it is not, in fact, a kind of freedom at all. In short, Locke thinks that we often use the term "freedom of will" or "free-will" to refer to what I am calling the Elusive Something. I will argue, then, that there is a sense in which Locke ultimately disagrees with the suggestion that the Elusive Something is freedom of will, and a sense in which he agrees. The sense in which he disagrees is this: He believes that no account of freedom of will that is recognizable as an account of a kind of freedom is the Elusive Something. The sense in which he agrees, however, is this: The Elusive Something—which he specifies in some detail—is what we often call "freedom of will" when we are speaking without philosophical rigor. So, there is a negative side to Locke's view in which he rejects a variety of accounts of the Elusive Something, accounts that are recognizable as accounts of *freedom* of will, and a positive side in which he offers his account of the Elusive Something, and—in the second and later editions—reluctantly agrees to call this extra something "freedom of will." In the next section, I look at the negative side of Locke's thoughts on the issue.

FREEDOM OF WILL: THE NEGATIVE VIEWS

Locke holds, officially at least, a strict view of philosophical language: He believes that in contexts in which language is to be used precisely, each word should unambiguously express a single, particular, well-defined idea. Despite the fact that he explicitly says that this is how philosophical language should work, he rarely rises to this standard himself; Locke is notorious for slipping on terminology. Nonetheless, he does espouse the belief that language should be used in this precise way. For instance:

> I know there are not Words enough in any Language to answer all the variety of Ideas, that enter into Men's discourses and rea- sonings. But this hinders not, but that when any one uses any term, he may have in his Mind a *determined* Idea, which he makes it the sign of, and to which he should keep it steadily annex'd during that present discourse. Where he does not, or cannot do this, he in vain pretends to *clear or distinct Ideas*: 'Tis plain his are not so: and therefore there can be expected nothing but obscurity and confusion, where such terms are made use of, which have not such a precise determination. ("Epistle to the Reader," p. 13)

There are a variety of places in the *Essay* in which this doc- trine plays an important role.[9] In general, the doctrine suggests a strategy for approaching philosophical questions: Start by giv- ing accounts of the ideas that the terms used in the question stand for, then go on to analyze the relationships between these ideas.

Locke takes himself to have given us an analysis of what idea the term "freedom" stands for (it stands for what I have called freedom of action), and an analysis of what the term "the will" stands for (it stands for the power to make choices, to engage in acts of will). So, it follows that the next step to take in under- standing whether or not the will is free is to apply these analyses by examining the relationship between the ideas that the terms stand for.

Free Wills

What Locke finds when he applies this strategy is that the question "Is the will free?" doesn't make sense when the terms "freedom" and "will" are given their precise philosophical readings. Even to try to describe the will as free requires that we think of the will as more than a particular power of the agent; it is to think of the will as a person within the person, or else some other discrete substance inside the agent. He says:

> 'Tis plain then, That the *Will* is nothing but one Power or Ability, and *Freedom* another Power or Ability: So that to ask, whether the *Will has Freedom*, is to ask, whether one Power has another Power, one Ability another Ability; a Question at first sight too grossly absurd to make a Dispute, or need an Answer. For who is it that sees not, that *Powers* belong only to *Agents*, and are *Attributes only of Substances, and not of Powers* themselves? So that this way of putting the Question, *viz.* whether the *Will be free*, is in effect to ask, whether the *Will* be a Substance, an Agent, or at least to suppose it, since Freedom can properly be attributed to nothing else. (II.XXI.16)

Notice that in this passage, Locke says that "this way of putting the Question, *viz.* whether the *Will be free*," involves a mistake. But this is to intimate that there might be another way of putting the question that does not involve such a mistake. That is, Locke hints, even here, that the question that we express when we ask about freedom of will might be expressible in a different way that does not involve the mistake he describes. Perhaps what Locke has in mind is that those who ask about freedom of the will are really asking about the Elusive Something. Therefore, there would be a way to ask about the Elusive Something without being misled by language by calling the Elusive Something "freedom of will." Be that as it may, Locke is, in the passage, making a substantive claim about what relations can and cannot hold between powers of the agent: in particular, powers do not have powers. But this stage of the argument is also marked by much discussion of what does and does not constitute proper, philosophically rigorous, speech. For instance:

The attributing to *Faculties* that which belonged not to them, has given occasion to this way of talking. . . . Not that I deny there are *Faculties*, both in the Body and Mind. . . . Nor do I deny, that those Words, and the like, are to have their place in the common use of Languages, that have made them currant. It looks like too much affectation wholly to lay them by: and Philosophy itself, though it likes not a gaudy dress, yet, when it appears in publick, must have so much Complacency, as to be cloathed in the ordinary Fashion and Language of the country, so far as it can consist with Truth and Perspicuity. (II.XXI.20)

What this passage suggests is that there is nothing wrong, in certain ordinary contexts, with speaking of freedom of will. The mistake is in taking that imprecise speech literally. But as Locke doesn't want to ban the imprecise usage of the term "freedom of will," he must think that some idea is expressed by the phrase; what bothers him is that the idea being expressed is not the idea that the words used in a precise and rigorous fashion express. What he is realizing is that the term "freedom of will" really signifies the Elusive Something, and he takes himself to have shown that the Elusive Something is badly described as "freedom of will," since that phrase just doesn't make literal sense.

To remedy the mistake of homunculizing the will—a mistake that the existence of the phrase "freedom of will" encourages— Locke thinks that we must always keep in mind that it is not a person's will that is free or unfree, but the person herself (cf. II.XXI.21). There might be ways, however, of avoiding this conclusion. We might, in particular, defend the claim that powers can have powers. Perhaps we would do this by granting an ontological status to powers that would make it coherent that they themselves could have powers without at the same time granting them the ontological status of substances.[10] But even if we accept that powers cannot have powers, how often do we really make the mistake of reifying the will? It might seem that Locke is making a quibbling point, he might seem to be pointing out a mistake that is only made by the philosophically careless, a mistake quite easy to avoid given even a modicum of philosophical sophistication. But, in fact, this is not so; it is a mistake that is very difficult not to make in thinking about freedom of will.

Certainly if I ask about the bondage of the will and in so doing I imagine a little person inside the person who is desperately trying, against the constraints of, for instance, bodily desire, to make a certain choice, I am making the mistake that Locke envisions. But, likely, I am making the same mistake in a large class of cases that might not seem at first glance to involve such a crude view of agency. For instance, the question "Could the agent have chosen differently from the way she did choose?" might involve the same mistake. One way of deciding whether or not I could have *acted* differently is to examine my environment in order to see whether or not there were aspects of my environment that ensured the occurrence of the action I performed independently of my choice to so act. This involves first deciding what was part of my environment and what was part of me; it involves thinking of me as separable from other factors relevant to the production of my actions. This separation of me from my environment is essential to the task at hand, for it seems that whether or not I could have acted differently depends on whether or not what I do depends on me rather than on factors external to me. If, in assessing whether or not I could have *chosen* differently, we start by thinking of various aspects of myself—such as my desires or my whims—that led to the choice that I made as being aspects of my environment, as being forces separable from myself, then we are conceiving of the self whose freedom is being assessed as merely the will, or merely reason, or merely the moral self; we are thinking of some aspect of the self as a self in its own right, the choosing-self, and thinking of other aspects of the self on the model of external circumstances. This move is only justified if whether or not I could have chosen otherwise depends on whether or not the choosing-self determines what I do rather than factors external to the choosing-self. But so long as we hold on to the idea that the choosing-self is merely a power of me rather than a substance within me, then whether or not I could choose differently simply cannot depend on whether or not the choosing-self determines what I do, for the choosing-self is not the sort of thing that is capable of action; it is not an agent, but a power.

If we take seriously the fact that my desires (or my values, or my higher order evaluations) are aspects of myself, then *any* role that they play in the production of choice is compatible with *me* bringing about the choice for exactly the same reason that I bring about an action when some aspect of me (namely, my choice) causes it to occur. There is, however, something about choices that makes them part of me in a deeper sense than that in which my desires are part of me—in fact, Locke offers an account of why this is so (see chapters 2 and 3)—and so it is wrong to say that any event that comes about as a result of any aspect of myself is one that was brought about by me. But it is tempting to give the explanation for the fact that choices are part of us in a stronger sense than desires—and therefore those things that come about as a result of an agent's choices are brought about by her in a way that those things brought about by other aspects of the agent are not—by thinking of the thing in which choices inhere as different from the thing in which desires inhere. That is, it is tempting to homunculize the will. But this is to avoid answering the deep question of what it is about choices that makes them part of ourselves in a way that desires—which are also just properties of the very same creature—are not; the issue is avoided through precisely the philosophical error that Locke is worried about, the reification of the will.

It often feels as though we are two (or more) selves. It often feels as though there is the desiring-self and the choosing-self and that the one is pushing the other toward particular choices. Sometimes it even feels as though there is a devil talking into one ear and an angel talking into the other. But we shouldn't take such feelings too seriously, for they encourage us to think of different aspects of ourselves as different individual selves. Locke's point is that it is quite natural to think of freedom of will as what we have when the choosing-self is capable of win-ning the war between itself and the desiring-self, or itself and the carnal-self. But if we take seriously the fact that the will is not a self, but an aspect of a larger self, it is wrong to characterize freedom of will in anything like this way.

If we accept Locke's initial metaphysical claim—that powers cannot have powers—then, in one fell swoop, Locke has ruled out of court a whole class of strategies for answering the question "Is the will free?" He has ruled out appeals to divisions within the mind, and appeals to the strength of the psychological aspects of a person—such as desires, values, or higher order evaluative attitudes—that usher in choice. Appeals to divisions within the mind require seeing one aspect of the mind (the moral-self, the will itself) as warring with some other aspect of the person (the desiring-self, the carnal-self). If the division between the opponents in this war, whatever they happen to be, is thought of as a substantial metaphysical division—if, that is, the parts of the self are thought of as substances—then we are reifying the mind's powers, thinking of them as substances in their own right. If, on the other hand, the sense in which the mind is divided is not metaphysical, but metaphorical, then we are likely to slip into thinking of the freedom of the will as turning on a battle between aspects of the agent's psyche. But if we are not careful, this conception involves a similar mistake: for an agent to have freedom of will, her will needn't actually win the war against her desires; it is sufficient that it could. But what does it mean to say that it could? There are two natural answers: The will has the power to overcome desire, or the agent has the power to overcome desire. The first answer involves the homunculization of the will, for only substances can have powers. The second, however, is an acceptable answer, but it amounts to a rather different question than "Is the will free?"; the question becomes "Are agents free to will?" and it is to that question that Locke turns next.

Locke, therefore, is neither asserting nor denying the freedom of the will in his objection to the coherence of the question "Is the will free?" Rather, he is discouraging us from thinking about the issue in a particular attractive way. He is discouraging us from thinking of the will as either the sort of thing that acts, or the sort of thing that is acted upon; the will is neither. What I have argued is that many of the most natural ways of thinking about freedom of will involve this mistake.

Free Volitions

But there is a way of asking the question "Is the will free?" that does not involve homunculizing the will, and does not simply reduce to the question "What is the Elusive Something?" Just as an agent's physical movements are either free or unfree—in the sense of freedom of action—by virtue of their relationship to choices (and hypothetical choices) on the part of the agent, the freedom or unfreedom of our volitions can be assessed by examining their relationship to other acts of will. Volitions, after all, are actions in a very broad sense—they are modifications of agents—and there is a meaningful sense in which actions are either free or unfree: agents do or do not have freedom of action with respect to them. So we can coherently ask whether or not the will is free by asking whether or not we possess freedom of action with respect to our choices.

It is instructive to look at the manner in which Locke introduces his discussion of this alternative way of asking whether or not the will is free. He says:

> [T]he inquisitive Mind of Man, willing to shift off from himself, as far as he can, all thoughts of guilt, though it be by putting himself into a worse state than that of fatal Necessity, is not content with this [that is, freedom of action]: Freedom, unless it reaches further than this, will not serve the turn: And it passes for a good Plea, that a Man is not free at all, if he be not as free to will as he is to act what he wills. (II.XXI.22)

Locke does two notable things in this passage. The first is to assert that "the inquisitive Mind of Man . . . is not content with" freedom of action; that is, he asserts that when we envision a truly free agent, we imagine a person who has more than just freedom of action, we envision an agent possessing the Elusive Something.[11] But, through his ironic tone, he also fore-shadows his rejection of a particular account of the Elusive

Something. The claim that he is about to reject is that an agent "is not free at all, if he be not as free to will as he is to act what he wills"; that is, he foreshadows his rejection of the claim that the Elusive Something consists in freedom of action with respect to volition.

In the sections following the section just quoted (sections 23–25), Locke argues that an agent's volitions are often not free; that is, in a large class of cases, agents simply lack freedom of action with respect to their volitions. He presents two arguments for this claim: one in sections 23 and 24, and a different argument in section 25. In the first, he describes a wide set of actions—those *"once proposed to [our] Thoughts, as presently to be done"* (II.XXI.23)—and argues that in these cases an agent's volition is not free (that is, the agent lacks freedom of action with respect to her volitions); in the second, he argues that the notion of a free volition only serves an account of the nature of (what we mistakenly call) freedom of will if we imagine an infinite series of acts of will. First, some remarks on the first argument.

Locke describes a rather common situation—a situation in which an agent does not consider performing a particular action until moments before that action must either be performed or not—and claims that when an agent faces such a situation, she lacks freedom of action with respect to her choice. Locke seems to think that when an agent is under time pressure (and believes herself to be), it is simply a conceptual truth that she will either choose or not choose; she cannot refrain from choosing entirely. However, as freedom of action consists in part in the ability to refrain voluntarily, an agent who cannot refrain from choosing lacks freedom of action with respect to choosing.[12] But putting aside the details of Locke's argument here, the important thing to notice is this: Examples of agents who lack freedom of action with respect to volition show nothing important if we think that the agents whom Locke describes lack the Elusive Something. That is, Locke is trying to refute the claim that the Elusive Something consists in freedom of action with respect to volition, and thereby refute the claim that the Elusive Something consists in a form of freedom of will (*properly* so called).[13] This claim is not refuted by a demonstration that some agents don't have freedom of action with respect to volition without also showing that at least some of those agents have the Elusive Something. However, the class of actions that Locke identifies—all of those that are in an agent's power and *"once proposed to his Thoughts, as presently to be done"* (II.XXI.23)— is sufficiently general to serve his purpose. After all, it just can't be that any agent who acts quickly in response to a proposal lacks the Elusive Something, lacks something essential to full-fledged free agency. In certain circumstances, time pressures might make us less than fully free agents, but it can't be that time pressures always do so, but, if Locke is right, certain time pressures always limit our freedom of action with respect to volition.

In the second argument for the claim that volitions are not free, Locke exploits his definition of freedom of action in a different way: For an act to be free, its occurrence must depend on a volition on the part of the agent in favor of that act. So, if an act of volition is free, it must have come about in accordance with a volition to have it, a volition to have a volition. This higher order volition can only be free if it too depended on a higher order volition to have it, and so on. Hence, either the agent has some volition that is not free (the highest order volition) or else we have to imagine an infinite series of volitions. Locke thinks the latter alternative ridiculous, but he does not explicitly engage with the former alternative. The former alternative, however, would not serve the purposes of someone trying to argue that the Elusive Something consists in freedom of volition: if it is necessary for an agent to have a free volition, that she have some higher order volition that is not free, then at the very least we need an explanation for why it is that the unfreedom of the highest order volition does not take freedom of will from the agent.

Locke, then, has offered an extended critique of the claim that the Elusive Something consists in some sort of freedom at the level of the will. He has argued that the will itself (that is, the power to engage in volitions) cannot be free—since the very idea involves reifying the will—and the actions of the will, choices, are not free in a large class of cases of agents who possess the Elusive Something. These claims together, if they are true, make the question, taken literally, "Is the will free?" rather irrelevant. Either the question just doesn't make sense, or else the answer to it just isn't important, for even if it turned out that our acts of will are free, we would be no closer to establishing that we possess the Elusive Something. We would be no closer, that is, to establishing that we are full-fledged free agents.

The interpretation that I am offering provides us with the tools necessary for interpreting the following puzzling remark:

> [H]ow can we think any one freer than to have the power to do what he will? . . . [W]e can scarce tell how to imagine any *Being* freer, than to be able to do what he *wills*. So that in respect of Actions, within the reach of such a power in him, a Man seems as free, as 'tis possible for Freedom to make him. (II.XXI.21)

There is a strong temptation to take this remark as simply stating a Hobbesean position on free agency: There is nothing more to full-fledged free agency than freedom of action. This interpretation, then, dismisses the rather vexing final flourish—stating that a person who has freedom of action is "as free, as 'tis possible for Freedom to make him"—as just an example (or, rather, another example!) of the unclarity that is so often the product of Locke's convoluted rhetorical style. But this rather uncharitable dismissal is unnecessary, for the remark means just what it says when Locke's position is taken as I am suggesting. An agent can approach full-fledged freedom through the possession of freedom of action, but she will get no closer to full-fledged freedom by giving her further forms of freedom—and, in particular, it will do no good to give her, literally, freedom of will. If she has freedom of action she is as free—that is, as close to being a full-fledged free agent—as she can be through the possession of something that is rightly called freedom: she is as free as freedom can make her. But this isn't to say that she couldn't be closer yet to being a full-fledged free agent; perhaps she could, but she would not become so by giving her any further kind of freedom, but only by giving her something else, something that, at this point in the chapter, Locke has yet to identify.

Given the assumption at Locke's time—an assumption that is, incidentally, still prevalent—that the Elusive Something just is freedom of will, the negative side of Locke's project was absolutely necessary. Before Locke could present his position as to the nature of the Elusive Something, he had to make clear that he was not attempting to offer an account of freedom of will. We might sum up Locke's negative views like this: The word "will" in the phrase "free will" can be given two interpretations: it could be expressing the idea of the power to make choices, or it could be expressing the idea of particular choices, acts of will. Interpreted in the former way, "free will" expresses the idea of a power of a power, and thus the idea expressed is incoherent. Interpreted in the latter way, "free will" expresses a coherent idea—freedom of action with respect to volition—but it fails to express the idea of that which we desire over and above freedom of action. Thus the prospects for a satisfying analysis of "free will" depend upon finding an alternative interpretation of "free." When we use the phrase "free will," we are not talking about a kind of freedom, strictly speaking; the word "free" is not expressing the idea of freedom of action. Thus, the way to assess Locke's positive account of the Elusive Something—to be examined in the next section—is not to see whether or not it tells us what we have when we have freedom of will, understood literally; we shouldn't expect the Elusive Something to be a kind of freedom. Rather, the right way to assess his account is to see whether agents who have what he claims the Elusive Something to be and also have freedom of action are really full-fledged free agents.

The Elusive Something and Freedom of Will: The Positive Views

Whatever the Elusive Something is, agents must have it or lack it by virtue of some fact—although what fact it is, we do not yet know—about their choices or volitions. When we consider an agent who has freedom of action, the natural thing to turn our attention to, when assessing whether or not she is really a full-fledged free agent, is her volition. Did her volition come about in the "right" way or did it come about as a result of addiction, indoctrination, coercion? What were the factors that determined her will? These are the right questions to ask when trying to decide whether or not an agent possesses the Elusive Something, and they are the right questions to ask precisely because the Elusive Something has something or other to do with the will. The question is what, exactly, with regard to the will an agent has when she has the Elusive Something. A first stab is to say that an agent who has the Elusive Something has the right kind of determination of volition. That is, a natural strategy to adopt in figuring out the nature of the Elusive Something is to first decide what it is that determines us to make the choices that we make and then go on to identify how the process through which we come to have our volitions can go "well" or go "badly." On this approach, an account of what it is, in fact, that determines our volitions will describe the process through which the volitions come about of both agents who possess and agents who lack the Elusive Something. That is, an account of the determination of volition will be relevant to, but not to be equated with, an account of the Elusive Something. It is natural to expect, then, that an account of the nature of the Elusive Something will rely on an account of what it is that determines us to have the volitions that we have, to make the choices that we make.

What, then, is Locke's view about the determination of volition? Between the first and second editions of the *Essay*, Locke changed his view in this regard and he, accordingly, changed his view about what it is in which the Elusive Something consists.

The First Edition

In the first edition, Locke's settled view is that an agent's will is determined by what appears to her to be the greatest good. What Locke means by this rests on his conception of what the greatest good is, so it is worth digressing briefly to explain what Locke takes the greatest good to be.

Locke held that where the right action is that action which accords with natural law—the law given by God—God also makes it the case that the right action is that action which maximizes the pleasure and minimizes the pain of the agent undertaking it. God creates this coincidence between the actions dictated by his laws and the actions that maximize any particular agent's pleasure by sentencing those who transgress his laws to lengthy (or perhaps eternal) torment in purgatory or hell, and those who obey them to an eternity of pleasure. Hence "the greatest good" is not exactly agent-relative for Locke. The greatest good for a particular agent is the maximization of the agent's personal pleasure, but the action that maximizes her personal pleasure is also the action that is best in a non-agent-relative sense, for God would only reward her with her greatest personal pleasure if she performs the action that accords with natural law, and God's laws would never require us to act in anything other than the best possible way. So, while there may be a conceptual distinction between what is best for the agent and what is best overall, there is no actual difference with respect to what an agent should do if she is to act in the best possible way. Hence, the greatest happiness (thought of as the maximization of pleasure and the minimization of pain) of a particular agent is, *from any agent's point of view*, the greatest good, for an agent can attain her own maximal happiness only if she performs the action that is in accord with God's law, and God—being benevolent—would not reward her for an action that did damage to the happiness of another. So, it is pointless to speculate about whether Locke means the good of the individual or the good of the aggregate of individuals, or what have you, when he uses the terms "the greatest good" or "the good," for God arranges things in such a way that all good things are achieved (to the degree to which it is possible for them to be achieved) when the agent acts in the way that maximizes her overall personal pleasure. In Locke's scheme, no matter whether we include only ourselves, or include all persons, or include only a subset of persons in the conception of the good that we allow to guide our conduct—provided our conception is accurate—we will do the same thing.[14]

Back to the determination of volition: It is noteworthy that at the beginning of Locke's discussion of the determination of volition in the first edition, he seems to be saying that the greatest good itself, not merely what appears to be the greatest good, determines the will. He says:

> [T]he cause of every less degree of Pain, as well as every greater degree of Pleasure, has the nature of Good, and *vice versa*, and is that which determines our Choice, and challenges our Preference. *Good* then, *the greater Good is that alone which determines the Will*. (II.XXI.29, first edition)

This is Locke's way of making the familiar Aristotelian-Scholastic point that the will aims at the good in something analogous to the way in which the understanding aims at the truth. However, the point is not expressive of Locke's settled first edition view of the determination of volition, for he realizes that if our volitions were really in general determined by the good itself, then all agents would reliably choose to do that action that would, in the long run, most contribute to their happiness. As this is not so, he concludes that the will is not always determined by the greatest good, but rather by what appears to be the greatest good. He says:

> *[T]hat which determines the choice* of the Will, and obtains the preference, *is still good, the greater Good:* But it is also only Good *that appears*; that which carries with it the Expectation of Addition to our Happiness, by the increase of our pleasures . . . or by the preventing, lessening, or shortning of pain. (II.XXI.38, first edition)

Further, because of our tendency to make mistaken comparisons between present and future pains and pleasures—we tend, that is, to underestimate future pleasures and pains when comparing them to present—it is not always the case that we do represent the greatest good to ourselves as such; what appears to us to be the greatest good is not always so (cf. II.XXI.38, first edition). This claim suggests that there might be an important difference between two kinds of agents: those whose judgments as to what is and is not good are correct and those who have mistaken judgments as to what is and is not good. (Locke does not draw a distinction between our judgments of the greatest good and what appears to us to be the greatest good. He believes, at the time of the first edition, that we judge to be the greatest good that which appears to us to be so, and vice versa.)[15]

Agents who have, nonaccidentally, accurate representations of the good have volitions that depend, in part, on what is, in fact, good.[16] That is, if I know that an agent has accurate representations of the good nonaccidentally, then figuring out what is in fact good is sufficient for figuring out what she does in fact choose. There is a sense, then, in which an agent of this sort has volitions that are "determined" by the good. Her volitions are not *causally* determined by the good—after all, the good might be a future state of happiness, and no event or state can cause an event or state that precedes it in time—but what volition she has depends, nonetheless, on what is, in fact, good. Her volitions are causally determined by her representations of the good—by what appears to her to be good—but her representations of the good, if they are accurate, depend for their content on what is, in fact, good.

Agents whose representations of the good are inaccurate—those who take things to be good that are not so either at all or to the degree that such agents take them to be—have volitions that are not "determined" by the good in the sense in which the volitions of the former sort of agent are. Agents of this second sort have volitions that are, we might say, "good independent": to figure out what such an agent will choose, it is of no use to figure out what is, in fact, good. If appealing to the nature of the good is the right way to explain the choice that the agent made, then the good did indeed "determine" the agent's choice. The agent's choice is caused by what appears to her to be good, but if we are to capture the important fact about some agents— namely, that what appears to them to be good is in fact so—we must make reference to the good itself and its correspondence with what the agent takes to be good when explaining the choice. Some agents have the beliefs that they have about where the good lies precisely because the good lies where they take it to lie, and in such agents the volitions that follow from their correct judgments are "determined" by the good.[17]

There are, thus, two senses of "determination" that we might have in mind when we ask what "determined" an agent's volition, and it is important to keep them straight: we might be asking about the immediate causal determinant of the volition, or we might be speaking of some fact (e.g., a fact about where the good lies) that serves to fix the choice that the agent makes. The distinction here can be thought of as a distinction between "caused by" on the one hand and "dependent on" on the other. If A is caused by B, then A is dependent upon B, but A could depend on B—could vary when B varies—without being caused by B.[18] Further, the fact that A depends on B doesn't rule out the possibility that A is caused by, say, C. Both could be true if something about C, crucial for the causation of A, depends, itself, on B. So, an agent's volition could be both caused by her judgment about where the good lies *and* dependent on the good itself, if she judges as she does precisely because the good lies where it lies. Dependency of one's volition on the good is a feature that one's volition can possess by virtue of features of the (determinant) efficient causal sequence through which one's volition comes about.

In the first edition, Locke is insistent that our choices are causally determined by what appears to us to be good—this is his first edition account of the determination of volition—but he also has the other kind of determination in mind when he speaks, as he does in the following passage, of steady determination by the good:

> If we look upon those *superior Beings* above us, who enjoy perfect Happiness, we shall have reason to judge that they are more stead-ily *determined in their choice of Good* than we; and yet we have no reason to think they are less happy, or less free, than we are. And if it were fit for such poor finite Creatures as we are to pronounce what infinite Wisdom and Goodness could do, I think, we might say, That God himself cannot choose what is not good; the Free-dom of the Almighty hinders not his being determined by what is best. (II.XXI.49; II.XXI.31, first edition)

The idea here is that the choices of God and angels are fixed by the evaluative facts, by the good (or, at least, are closer to being so fixed than ours). Locke doesn't presume to offer an account of the causal mechanics through which the choices of God and angels come about, as he is willing to do in our case. But he is clear that to have one's choices "steadily determined" by the good—that is, dependent upon the good—is not to *lack* any kind of freedom. This point is emphasized further in the following passage:

> Is it worth the Name of *Freedom* to be at liberty to play the Fool and draw Shame and Misery upon a Man's self? If to break loose from the conduct of Reason, and to want that restraint of Examination and Judgment, which keeps us from chusing or doing the worse, be *Liberty*, true Liberty, mad Men and Fools are the only Freemen: But yet, I think, nobody would chuse to be mad for the sake of such *Liberty*, but he that is mad already. (II.XXI.50; II.XXI.32, first edition)

The claim of both of these passages is that a creature whose volitions are determined by the good itself is not unfree in any respect whatsoever. Locke holds, therefore, that agents are not unfree when their volitions are determined by, dependent on, something external to themselves: the good itself. What this implies is that Locke is denying that an agent is free when and only when she is the sole source of her conduct—when and only when, that is, her conduct depends on nothing but herself—for the fact that an agent's choice depends upon something external to herself (namely, the good) does not undermine her freedom.

There is no explicit claim in the passages just quoted as to the nature of the Elusive Something. But, in fact, Locke has an account in mind:

> A Man is at liberty to lift up his Hand to his Head, or let it rest quiet: He is perfectly indifferent to either; and it would be an imperfection in him, if he wanted that Power, if he were deprived of that Indifferency. But it would be as great an imperfection, if he had the same Indifferency, whether he would prefer the lifting up his Hand, or its remaining in rest, when it would save his Head

or Eyes from a blow he sees coming: *'tis* as much *a perfection, that the power of Preferring should be determined by Good,* as that the power of Acting should be determined by the Will; and the certainer such determination is, the greater is, the perfection. (II.XXI.30, first edition)

Locke describes here two "perfections" that a person can have. The first is freedom of action, the determination of action or absence of action (that is, causation of action or absence of action, and thus dependency) in accordance with the agent's will. The second is the determination (in the sense of dependency only) of an agent's volition—her "preference," as he often calls volition—by the good. What role is this second perfection intended to play in Locke's account? I suggest that Locke intends the second perfection to be an account of the Elusive Something. He is offering an account of what it is that "the inquisitive mind of man" is really after, over and above freedom of action. Just as we want there to be robust ties between our volitions and our actions, we want there to be robust ties between our choices and the good. Freedom of action is a kind of perfection in the causal determination of action: an agent has it when her action is determined (in both senses) by her volition, and an incompatible action would have occurred had she willed it. The Elusive Something, then, is a perfection in the causal determination of volition: an agent has it when her volitions are causally determined by (nonaccidentally) correct judgments as to what is good, judgments the content of which depend on what is, in fact, good—when, that is, her volitions are dependent upon the good itself.

I take it, then, that at the time of the first edition, Locke held the following view:

> *The Elusive Something, First Edition*: An agent has the Elusive Something *if and only if* the agent has the second perfection *if and only if* the agent's volition is determined by (dependent on) what is, in fact, the greatest good.

I don't mean to suggest that this interpretation is clearly implied by the evidence so far cited. After all, there is nothing in the first edition to suggest that Locke explicitly recognized dependency of volition on the good to be a part of full-fledged free agency. He does treat it as a perfection analogous to freedom of action, but he doesn't describe it explicitly as that which is required over and above freedom of action for full-fledged freedom. As we'll see in the next section, however, this suggested interpretation of the first edition gains credence when we see how Locke develops his view in the later editions of the *Essay*.

It is a consequence of the first edition account of the Elusive Something that no agent who makes a wrong choice was, at the time, a full-fledged free agent. If an agent makes the wrong choice, and consequently does the wrong action, an action that will contribute (eventually) to her long-term pain (inflicted through extended punishment in the afterlife), then her choice was certainly not determined by the good, since the content of her judgment was not decided by the nature of the good. Her volition was caused by her judgments of what was good, but as her judgments were mistaken, her choice was not determined by the good itself. What this implies is that in the first edition, whether he knows it or not, Locke is detaching full-fledged free agency from moral responsibility. He has an account of the Elusive Something, and thereby an account of full-fledged free agency: An agent is a full-fledged free agent when she has both perfections, when she has freedom of action, and determination of volition by the good. But Locke could not plausibly hold that an agent need be a full-fledged free agent in order to be justly held responsible for her wrong choices and actions, since his account would then imply that no agent who chooses wrongly is justly held responsible for her wrong choice.

In a letter to Locke, written after the publication of the first edition and before the publication of the second, Molyneux criticized the first edition account of free agency. He says:

[Y]ou seem to make all Sins to proceed from our Understandings, or to be against Conscience; and not at all from the Depravity of our Wills. Now it seems harsh to say, that a Man shall be Damn'd, because he understands no better than he does.[19]

Under the first edition account of what it is that causally determines the will, an agent who has wrong volitions (that is, volitions to do wrong) has them by virtue of having made a wrong judgment, that is, by virtue of having a mistaken belief about which of her alternative actions promises the most pleasure and the least pain (in the long run). Molyneux's point is that it follows from Locke's first edition view that all agents who make a wrong choice, have a wrong volition, do so by virtue of having a mistaken judgment.[20] However, judgments are products of the understanding, not the will—in contemporary terms, they have the "direction of fit" of beliefs rather than desires, intentions or choices—and, hence, they do not express anything "depraved" about the agent's will.[21]

Molyneux's criticism is not exactly on the mark. After all, Locke does not think that we are to be held responsible for actions that are not voluntary, and voluntary actions are those that satisfy volitions, our acts of will. Hence, voluntary evil actions are expressive of evil volitions (where an evil volition is just a volition to do an evil thing), and surely if an agent has evil volitions, there is something depraved about her will. At the very least, we could say of an agent who acts wrongly as a result of a choice so to act that she is a bad-chooser, and insofar as the will is just the power to make choices, being a bad-chooser is one way in which one's will might be depraved. More importantly, Locke thinks that agents make many mistaken judgments as a result of their voluntary actions or through negligence. Hence, many mistaken judgments are themselves expressive of "depravity" in the agent's will. He says:

> Judging is, as it were, balancing an account, and determining on which side the odds lie. If therefore either side be hudled up in haste, and several of the Sums that should have gone into the reckoning be overlook'd, and left out, this Precipitancy causes as *wrong a Judgment*, as if it were a perfect Ignorance. . . . To check this Precipitancy, our Understanding and Reason were given us, if we will make a right use of them, to search, and see, and then judge thereupon. . . . How much sloth and negligence, heat and

passion, the prevalency of fashion, or acquired indispositions, do severally contribute, on occasion, to these *wrong Judgments*, I shall not here further inquire. (II.XXI.44, first edition; II.XXI.67, second and later editions)

We end up with mistaken judgments when out of sloth or negligence we deliberate too quickly and without sufficient care. Errors of this sort express depravity not in our understandings, but in our wills: an agent is held responsible for a poor choice arising out of a mistaken judgment in such a case in part because it is her own fault that she has made a mistaken judgment. In short, there are two ways in which, even in Locke's first edition account, the action of an agent who chooses to do the wrong thing—the action that, because it violates natural law, will lead in the end to the agent's long-term or eternal discomfort in the afterlife—expresses depravity of will: It can express depravity of will in the weak sense in which an agent's will is "depraved" just in case she makes wrong choices, and in a further sense in which the agent's wrong judgment can be traced to some sort of negligence on her part, some failure to choose rightly on an earlier occasion. The earlier choice would express depravity in the agent's will only in the first sense—presuming that her sloth or negligence was not itself due to some prior sloth or negligence—but, nonetheless, when her wrong choice arises out of a wrong judgment for which we can blame her, depravity in the agent's will is doubly expressed.

But Molyneux's point is not entirely off the mark. A large number of wrong choices are made as a result of mistaken judgments that do not come about as a result of any fault in the agent's will, any sloth or negligence on the part of the agent. If, for instance, I have had a poor education, I may make a mistaken judgment without being rightly charged with sloth or negligence of the requisite sort; I just don't know any better, as it were. In such cases, my action expresses "depravity of will" only by virtue of the fact that it expresses a depraved volition. But perhaps the having of evil volitions is not enough to show that an agent's will is depraved in the manner that it would need to be in order to justify judgments of responsibility. We might say of such an agent that she is ignorant or mistaken when she chooses as she does, but not that she is evil. In short, what Molyneux's challenge suggests is that Locke needs to say something more nuanced about a large class of actions and agents than he has said in the first edition. As Molyneux himself put it, Locke's first edition account was too "fine spun":[22] a fabric made from thread spun too finely lacks richness of texture. To answer Molyneux's worry, Locke needs a more textured account of the differences between agents who act wrongly.

Molyneux's criticism, then, offers Locke a challenge: He must draw some deeper distinctions among cases in which agents have the wrong volitions than he has drawn in the first edition account. In fact, Locke agreed that his account needed more texture, and responded to Molyneux by saying that he had suspected all along that his account was "too fine spun."[23] In the second (and later) editions, Locke tries to come up to the challenge by offering a subtler account of what it is that causally determines us to have the volitions that we have, an account that would allow him to make a wider range of distinctions among various kinds of agents who act wrongly. Just as Locke's first edition account of the Elusive Something was linked to his account of what causally determines us to have the acts of volition that we have—the Elusive Something was perfection in such causal determination—his new account of the Elusive Something arises out of his new account of what causally determines the will.

The Second and Later Editions

In the second and later editions, Locke starts to call agents who possess the second perfection "free" as a result. And in fact, in places, he seems to say that agents who have the second perfection have freedom of will, although he is careful to point out that it is a mistake to call it that. Consider, for instance, Locke's addition to the second edition following the first edition passage stating his view as to the nature of the second perfection. The first edition passage, recall, reads as follows:

> A Man is at liberty to lift up his Hand to his Head, or let it rest quiet: He is perfectly indifferent to either; and it would be an imperfection in him, if he wanted that Power, if he were deprived of that Indifferency. But it would be as great an imperfection, if he had the same Indifferency, whether he would prefer the lifting up his Hand, or its remaining in rest, when it would save his Head or Eyes from a blow he sees coming: *'tis* as much *a perfection, that the power of Preferring should be determined by Good*, as that the power of Acting should be determined by the Will; and the certainer such determination is, the greater is, the perfection. (II.XXI.30, first edition)[24]

In the second and later editions, this passage is followed with the following remark:

> [W]ere [our volitions] determined by anything but the last result of our own Minds, judging of the good or evil of any action, we were not free, the very end of our Freedom being, that we might attain the good we chuse. (II.XXI.48)[25]

Locke says here that some form of freedom is lacking in agents whose volitions are not determined appropriately, but what kind of freedom can he have in mind? Locke cannot be speaking here of freedom of action, for an agent can have freedom of action regardless of what determines her to have the volition that she has. He can only be speaking of some kind of freedom beyond freedom of action, and he seems to think that an agent lacks such freedom when her volitions are not determined appropriately. The kind of freedom (imprecisely speaking) undermined by the wrong kind of determination of volition can only be freedom of will.

Another passage that illustrates Locke's willingness in the second and later editions to call the second perfection a kind of freedom occurs in his recapitulation of the argument toward the end of the chapter:

The result of our judgment upon . . . Examination is what ultimately determines the Man, who could not be *free* if his *will* were
determin'd by any thing, but his own *desire* guided by his own
Judgment. (II.XXI.71)

Again, why should Locke think that any kind of freedom is undermined in an agent whose volitions are determined inappro-
priately if he also believes that the only sort of freedom is freedom of action? He has recognized, by the time of the second
edition, that his account of the Elusive Something—that is, the
second perfection—is an account of just that: it is an account
of what a full-fledged free agent has over and above freedom of
action.

There are additional passages that illustrate (perhaps more
clearly) Locke's increasing willingness in the second and later
editions to talk of the Elusive Something as integral to free
agency, as, even, a kind of freedom. In fact, in places he is willing to call the Elusive Something "freedom of will," although
he is careful to add the clause "improperly so called." As these
same passages illustrate not just that Locke equates the second
perfection—and thereby the Elusive Something—with freedom of will, but also indicate the changes to the first edition
account of the nature of the Elusive Something, I save my discussion of them for later.

As I mentioned, different accounts of what it is that causally
determines an agent to choose as she does will suggest different
accounts of the Elusive Something, different accounts, that is,
of what perfection in such causal determination amounts to. As
Locke changes his account of what it is that causes our volitions
in the second and later editions, he also changes his account of
the nature of the Elusive Something. In the second and later
editions, Locke claims that our volitions are caused by "uneasinesses." Uneasinesses are a species of pain, a feeling of dissatis-
faction with one's current state. Uneasinesses take objects; an
agent feels uneasy because she recognizes that she is lacking
something, but this "recognition" needn't be a belief of some
sort; uneasinesses are often inarticulate pains crying to be re-
lieved by attainment of some object. (All of these various claims

emerge in II.XXI.31.) An agent can feel many different uneasinesses at once, and it follows that different volitions are dictated
by different uneasinesses: depending on what the agent feels
she lacks, she will be moved toward different actions as the appropriate actions for quelling her uneasiness. There is a relation
of precedence among uneasinesses: the uneasiness that is "the
most pressing" at a particular time is the one that causes the
agent to have a particular volition, a volition to act in a manner
that will relieve that uneasiness:

> [W]e being in this World beset with sundry *uneasinesses*, distracted
> with different *desires*, the next inquiry naturally will be, which of
> them has the precedency in determining the *will* to the next
> action? and to that the answer is, that ordinarily, which is the
> most pressing of those that are judged capable of being then
> removed . . . [T]he most important and urgent *uneasiness* we at
> that time feel, is that, which ordinarily determines the *will*.
> (II.XXI.40)

As uneasiness is a species of pain, and happiness, in Locke's
view, is the greatest pleasure and absence of pain, the removal
of uneasinesses is necessary for happiness (cf. II.XXI.36). But,
things are complicated, for we may need to refrain from reliev-
ing one particular uneasiness now in order to relieve a greater
one later; that is, we might need to defer present pleasure for
the sake of greater future pleasure. We can determine whether
or not this is so—we can contemplate future and greater goods
and see that to pursue what we are now uneasy in the want of
might interfere with getting those greater goods—and when
we do so carefully, we raise uneasiness in ourselves for those
future greater goods:

> We are seldom at ease, and free enough from the solicitation of
> our natural or adopted desires, but a constant succession of *uneasi-
> nesses* out of that stock which natural wants or acquired habits
> have heaped up, take the *will* in their turns; and no sooner is one
> action dispatch'd, which by such a determination of the *will* we
> are set upon, but another *uneasiness* is ready to set us on work.
> For the removing of the pains we feel, and are at present pressed

with, being the getting out of misery, and consequently the first
thing to be done in order to happiness, absent good, though
thought on, confessed, and appearing to be good, not making
any part of this unhappiness in its absence, is jostled out, to make
way for the removal of those *uneasinesses* we feel, till due, and repeated Contemplation has brought it nearer to our Mind, given
some relish of it, and raised in us some desire; which then beginning to make a part of our present *uneasiness*, stands upon fair
terms with the rest to be satisfied, and so, according to its great-
ness and pressure, comes in its turn to determine the *will*.
(II.XXI.45)[26]

"Due, and repeated Contemplation" of future goods raises in
us uneasinesses for those future goods in proportion to their
value: the amount of pleasure (and absence of pain) that they
promise. These uneasinesses compete with our present-di-
rected uneasiness in causal determination of the will. So, contemplation of the relevant sort—in other passages, Locke refers
to such contemplation as "deliberation" (cf. II.XXI.52)—can
play a role in the determination of volition: in the absence of
such contemplation, an agent would have had different uneasinesses and, hence, a different volition.

Notice that what Locke refers to here as "contemplation"
and occasionally as "deliberation" is only one aspect of what we
usually think of as deliberation. A standard picture of deliberation is this: deliberation is motivated by an uncertainty about
which of our alternative actions is the best action. That is, we
enter into deliberation without any particular beliefs about
which of our alternative actions are the best ones. The activity
of deliberation, then, is aimed in part, and only in part, at gaining such beliefs. This activity is quite complicated; in deliberation the agent both bestows evaluative weights on outcomes
that she did not antecedently evaluate, and introspects to determine how she already weights other outcomes. Further, evaluations of consequences are hardly the only attitudes that seem
to be involved: an agent also takes into account her conception
of herself and her beliefs about who she should be. But, however the mechanics work, part of what we gain from delibera-

tion is a belief about which action of the alternatives is the best one. But as deliberation is practical, we gain more than just beliefs: at the end of deliberation, we make choices and form intentions, we gain mental states that are efficacious in the production of action.

Locke does not reject this picture, exactly, but he thinks of deliberation a little bit differently. At least in the second and later editions, the part of deliberation that leads to beliefs about which of one's alternative actions is best (that is, judgments) is merely a process of reasoning about probable consequences, and estimating the amount of pleasure and pain that they promise. There is nothing *practical* about this aspect of the process: it is not different from reasoning about any other future matter of fact given information about the past. It is just a form of inductive inference leading, as all inductive inference does, to beliefs about future matters of fact. Locke frequently uses the term "deliberation"—although he more often uses the term "contemplation"—to describe not mere probabilistic reasoning about future pleasures and pains, but to refer, rather, to an activity that begins after one has already developed beliefs about which of one's alternative actions promises the greatest good: this further activity is not a kind of reasoning at all; it is, rather, an imaginative process through which we translate our beliefs about the greatest good into feelings, uneasinesses, the kinds of things that can actually bring about choices. This is the process of "due, and repeated Contemplation" (II.XXI.45) through which we make future pleasures and pains—and particularly the pleasures and pains of the afterlife—alive to ourselves.

This dual conception of deliberation deserves emphasis. For Locke, determining which of one's alternative actions is best is a matter of determining which possible action promises the greatest pleasure for oneself. Once one has determined that, one has made a "judgment" about which action is best. But, in the second and later editions, Locke thinks that such judgments are inert in the production of choices. He seems to think that the idea that judgments could cause volitions violates constraints of "action at a distance":

Another reason why 'tis *uneasiness* alone determines the will, may
be this. Because that alone is present, and, 'tis against the nature
of things, that what is absent should operate, where it is not. It
may be said, that absent good may by contemplation be brought
home to the mind, and made present. The *Idea* of it indeed may
be in the mind, and view'd as present there: but nothing will be
in the mind as a present good, able to counter-balance the removal of any *uneasiness*, which we are under, till it raises our desire,
and the *uneasiness* of that has the prevalency in determining the
will. (II.XXI.37)

The idea here seems to be this: The will is affected only by
present pleasure and pain, good and evil. Judgments about future pleasures and pains are not themselves pleasurable or painful, for the future pleasures and pains are in the mind, when we
make a judgment, only as representations, as ideas, not as actual
pains or pleasures. It follows that judgments about future pleasures and pains cannot by themselves have any effect on the
mind. Insofar as standard deliberative processes, reasonings
about cause and effect, deliver to us only ideas of future pleasures and pains, such deliberation is not genuinely practical: it
does not result in determinations of the will. For a choice to be
caused, for us to make a choice that accords with our judgments,
we need to do something further: we need to "contemplate"
future goods and evils, pleasures and pains, and raise appropriate uneasinesses, pains, in ourselves in accordance with those
future pleasures and pains.[27] In the first stage of deliberation,
we reach judgments; in the second, we turn the future pleasures
and pains that we judge to follow from various alternative actions into present pains, uneasinesses.[28]

Notice, then, that because deliberation, or "contemplation,"
is voluntary action—the agent chooses to imagine, to contemplate, future pleasures and pains and thereby raise uneasinesses
in herself that are appropriate to them—Locke has given the
agent's will a role in the determination of volition. Or, at least,
he has given the agent's will a possible role in the causal determination of volition. Say an agent has freedom of action with
respect to such deliberation—she will deliberate if she so

chooses, and she'll do something incompatible with deliberating if she chooses to do that instead. Imagine that she does deliberate, alters her uneasiness in accordance with her judgments about future goods and evils, and thereby alters her volition to act (not to be confused with her volition to deliberate) from what it would have been in the absence of such deliberation. In such a case, the agent's volition to act was caused in part by an act of her will: her volition to deliberate. On the other hand, imagine that she does not deliberate in this manner and her volition to act is caused by her present uneasinesses— a set of uneasinesses that may or may not include uneasinesses that are in accord with her judgments about future pleasures and pains. In such a case, the agent's volition to act is caused in part by the absence of a relevant act of will: had she had a volition to deliberate, she would have deliberated and thereby altered her uneasinesses.

Since the second edition account of the causes of volition provides for the possibility that the will can affect itself through deliberation, it suggests a natural first account of the Elusive Something:

> *The Elusive Something, Second Edition, First Try*: An agent has the Elusive Something *if and only if* the agent has freedom of action with respect to deliberation.

Under this "First Try" at Locke's account of the Elusive Something, Locke's view falls prey to an objection pointed out by Michael Ayers:[29] As deliberation is intentional action, it arises out of volition, so we can ask whether or not the agent had the Elusive Something with regard to deliberation; we can ask, that is, whether the agent could have deliberated about whether or not to deliberate. If the answer is "yes," then we can go one step toward a regress by asking whether or not the agent could have deliberated about whether or not to deliberate about whether or not to deliberate. On the other hand, if the agent was not able to deliberate about whether or not to deliberate, then, according to the "First Try," she did not possess the Elusive Something with respect to deliberation, and as a consequence, she was not a full-fledged free agent with respect to the act of deliberating. She had only freedom of action when she deliberated about whether or not to act; she lacked it with respect to deliberation about whether or not to deliberate. But, if we thought that freedom of action with respect to deliberation was important for assessing whether or not the agent was a full-fledged free agent with respect to the action, then, at the very least, we need an explanation for why it is that the agent does not also need the freedom to deliberate about whether or not to deliberate to have full freedom with respect to the action. Without such an explanation, we have a regress: the agent needs not just the ability to deliberate in order to have full freedom with respect to action, she also needs the ability to deliberate about whether or not to deliberate and the ability to deliberate about whether or not to deliberate about whether or not to deliberate, and so on.

Notice the similarity of this objection to Locke's own objection—the objection stated in II.XXI.25—to the claim that freedom of will (and thereby the Elusive Something) consists in having freedom of action with respect to the relevant act of volition. Locke objected that since the freedom of an act (any act, whether an act of the mind like volition or a physical action) consists in dependency on a prior volition, an act of volition can only be free if either there is some volition (the highest order volition) that is not free, or else an infinite regress of volitions. This objection only has bite if we lack an explanation of why it is that we need freedom beyond freedom of action with respect to all the relevant volitions (the volition to have a volition to act, and the volition to have a volition to have a volition to act, etc.) and not just freedom of action with respect to the last volition before action in order to have freedom of will with respect to the action. The point is this:

Consider a theory of freedom of will with the following structure: An agent has freedom of will with respect to A *if and only if* her volition to A, V_0, bears relation R to another volition V_1.[30] The earlier theory that Locke considers and rejects—that freedom of will consists in freedom of action with respect to volition—is an example of such a view (under Locke's account of freedom of action): An agent has freedom of will with respect to A when V_0 bears the relationship to V_1 that A bears to V_0 (assuming the agent had freedom of action with respect to A). Locke rejected this account on the grounds that such an account gives rise to a regress: we have as much reason to ask about the relationship of V_0 to V_1 as we have to ask about the relationship of V_1 to V_2 and V_2 to V_3 and so on. However, the view of the Elusive Something, of freedom of will mistakenly so called, captured in the "First Try" is also an example of such a theory: V_0 is a volition to A, V_1 is a volition to deliberate about whether or not to have V_0, V_2 is a volition to deliberate about whether or not to have V_1, and so on. Ayers objects to this theory on the same grounds that Locke objected to the earlier theory: We lack an explanation for why it would be satisfactory for there to be a last volition in the sequence—a volition that did not bear the relationship to any further volition that it itself bears to some volition earlier in the sequence. But without such an explanation, we have a regress.

As Locke objected to the earlier theory—under which freedom of will (and hence the Elusive Something) consists in freedom of action with respect to volition—on grounds exactly analogous to those on which Ayers objects to Locke, it is somewhat implausible to suggest that Locke held the view of freedom of will described in the "First Try," for Locke never even engaged with the Ayers objection; since he voiced the objection against the earlier suggestion, it is somewhat strange that he would overlook it in his own case. Of course, he may have done so, and, to be sure, there are texts that make it sound like the "First Try" at the Elusive Something is what Locke had in mind. For instance:

> [T]he mind having in most cases, as is evident in Experience, a power to *suspend* the execution and satisfaction of any of its desires; and so all, one after another; is at liberty to consider the objects of them; examine them on all sides, and weigh them with others. In this lies the liberty Man has; and from the not using of it right comes all that variety of mistakes, errors, and faults which

we run into in the conduct of our lives, and our endeavours after
happiness; whilst we precipitate the determination of our *wills*,
and engage too soon, before due *Examination*. To prevent this, we
have a power to *suspend* the prosecution of this or that desire; as
every one daily may Experiment in himself. This seems to me the
source of all liberty; in this seems to consist that which is (as I
think improperly) call'd *Free-Will*. (II.XXI.47)

A first point to note about this passage is Locke's willingness
to speak here of a kind of freedom over and above freedom of
action and his striking statement that this kind of freedom is
what is "improperly call'd *Free-Will*." Locke can only be speaking here of the Elusive Something: "In this"—and I will discuss
shortly what "this" is—"lies the liberty Man has." He is describing the extra conditions that an agent must satisfy if she is to
be a full-fledged free agent, and he is willing to say that this is
what we (mistakenly call) free will. In short, he is explicitly offering an account of the Elusive Something and he is equating
the Elusive Something with (what we mistakenly call) freedom
of will.

But to return to the point at hand: On the table was a particular claim—what I called the "First Try"—as to what the Elusive
Something (that is, what we mistakenly call freedom of will) is
in the second edition. The passage just quoted seems to be an
explicit statement that an agent who has the power to suspend
the effect of uneasinesses in the determination of the will and
who (thereby) has the power to deliberate—to examine her uneasinesses and raise uneasinesses in herself in accordance with
her judgments as to future pleasure and pain—has (what is mistakenly called) freedom of will, has, that is, the Elusive Something.[31] But the passage needs to be considered with some care,
because it is possible that Locke invokes the power to suspend
and deliberate because it is through the exercise of that power
that we are able to bring it about that we have the Elusive
Something; that is, it is possible that he takes the Elusive Something not to consist in the power to suspend and deliberate but
to consist in something else that is *gained* through suspension
and deliberation. But what is gained through suspension and

deliberation? One of the things that Locke takes to be gained is accordance between one's volitions and one's judgments. Perhaps he takes such accordance to be the Elusive Something:

> *The Elusive Something, Second Edition, Second Try*: An agent has the Elusive Something *if and only if* her volitions accord with her judgments, or she has the power to bring it about that her volitions accord with her judgments.

And, indeed, Locke does frequently speak as though this is what is required, over and above freedom of action for full-fledged freedom (cf. II.XXI.71, quoted earlier). Nonetheless, I don't think that the "Second Try" is what Locke has in mind. Although the strongest arguments against the "Second Try" will appear in the course of the discussion, at this point it is worth noting that Locke, in fact, explicitly describes his interest in suspension for the sake of deliberation in the section immediately preceding his description, at II.XXI.47, of that which is "call'd *Free-Will*," and he does not describe the function of suspension and deliberation to be the elimination of conflict, or the production of accordance, between volition and judgment. He says:

> For good, though appearing and allowed ever so great, yet till it has raised desires in our Minds, and thereby made us *uneasie* in its want, it reaches not our *wills*; we are not within the Sphere of its activity, our *wills* being under the determination only of those *uneasinesses* which are present to us, which (whilst we have any) are always soliciting, and ready at hand to give the *will* its next determination. (II.XXI.46)

To raise an uneasiness in oneself (as we do in deliberation) in accordance with one's judgment about a future good is to allow one's will to be determined by the good itself. The good itself does not act on the will—we are not within its "the Sphere of its activity"—until we raise an uneasiness in ourselves for that which is good. So, the point of deliberation of the sort under discussion is that when we deliberate, we allow our wills to be determined by the good. For all that Locke says here, there would be no real point to bringing one's volitions in accordance with one's judgments, unless, by doing so, one thereby brought about accordance between one's volition and the good. So, Locke invokes the power to suspend the effect of desire in order to deliberate, because he thinks that through such deliberation, we bring it about that our wills are determined by the good. He is elaborating on the account of the Elusive Something offered in the first edition by explicating the role that deliberation plays in bringing it about that an agent's will is determined in the way it needs to be for her to be a full-fledged free agent.

Here, then, is a third alternative (and, as I will argue, a better) interpretation of what Locke takes, in the second and later editions, to be the Elusive Something, to be, that is, (what we mistakenly call) freedom of will:

> *The Elusive Something, Second Edition, Third Try*: An agent has the Elusive Something *if and only if* an agent has (what we mistakenly call) freedom of will *if and only if* either her volitions are determined by the good, or she has the power to bring it about that her volitions are determined by the good.[32]

The change in the account of the causal determination of volition from the first to the second edition yields a role that deliberation can play in the causation of volition: deliberation can shape uneasinesses and thereby shape volitions. Hence, an agent can either have the Elusive Something for the same reasons that she had it in the first edition—because her volitions are determined by the good—or she can have it because she had the power to bring it about that her volitions were so determined.[33] What Locke has realized between the first and second editions is that there is a way in which an agent can bring it about that her volitions are determined appropriately. In the first edition, he didn't realize that this was possible, for he didn't see a mechanism by which we could adjust those psychic elements (judgments, in the first edition) that cause volition. In the second edition, he has come to realize—as a result of his change in view as to the causal determination of volition—that there is an activity (deliberation, contemplation) that can serve to adjust our volitions to the good by adjusting the causal determinants of volition (uneasinesses).

Locke seems to think that we have the power to bring it about that our volitions are determined by the good just in case we have freedom of action with respect to deliberation. That is, he doesn't seem to think that there are other mechanisms by which we can adjust our volitions to match the good, other mechanisms by which we can make the content of our volitions depend on the nature of the good itself. However, Locke seems to think that, for all we know, other creatures might have very different mechanisms for bringing it about that their volitions are determined by the good, and this would not detract from their freedom. That is, there is nothing about deliberation per se that is essential to freedom—as the "First Try" seems to suggest—nor is there anything essential to freedom about bringing about accordance between volition and judgment—as the "Second Try" suggests. The only feature of deliberation (and the consequent accordance between volition and judgment that it produces) that makes it essential to possessing the Elusive Something is that through it we are able to adjust our volitions so that they match the good. We can see that this is so from Locke's remarks about the freedom of God and angels, quoted earlier:

> If we look upon those *superior Beings* above us, who enjoy perfect Happiness, we shall have reason to judge that they are more steadily *determined in their choice of Good* than we; and yet we have no reason to think they are less happy, or less free, than we are. And if it were fit for such poor finite Creatures as we are to pronounce what infinite Wisdom and Goodness could do, I think, we might say, That God himself cannot choose what is not good; the Freedom of the Almighty hinders not his being determined by what is best. (II.XXI.49; II.XXI.31, first edition)

As I mentioned before, this passage is evidence primarily for seeing Locke as claiming that determination of choice by the good does not take away from freedom. However, mention of deliberation is conspicuously absent from this passage as is mention of any kind of accordance between the judgments of God or angels and their volitions. There is no intimation here that the freedom of God and angels rests on their freedom of action with respect to deliberation or their power to produce accordance between volition and judgment. And, in fact, in another passage Locke is very careful to say that it is finite beings such as ourselves that are full-fledged free agents by virtue of the fact that we can suspend the effects of our uneasinesses and deliberate:

> This, as seems to me is the great privilege of finite intellectual Beings; and I desire it may be well consider'd, whether the great inlet and exercise of all the *liberty* Men have . . . does not lie in this, that they can *suspend* their desires, and stop them from determining their *wills* to any action, till they have duly and fairly *examin'd* the good and evil of it, as far forth as the weight of the thing requires. (II.XXI.52)

Insofar as it is only finite creatures who are full-fledged free agents when they have freedom of action with respect to deliberation, such freedom of action must be only contingently associated with the Elusive Something, with freedom of will. But then these two passages give us reason to reject the interpretation in the "First Try." (The second passage is indeterminate with respect to the "Second Try.") When our volitions are determined by the good—either because we exercise our power to deliberate or else naturally through, we might say, divine grace[34]—we have something in common with God and angels. However, we are also different from God and angels in a crucial respect: We sometimes fail to use our freedom of action with respect to deliberation in cases in which we need to if our volitions are to be determined by the good, and in such cases our volitions fail to be determined in the way that they should. The fact that we are endowed in certain circumstances with freedom of action with respect to deliberation is our "great privilege," because it is through its use that we are able to bring it about that our volitions are determined by the good, just like the volitions of God and angels.

Another piece of evidence for my interpretation comes from a passage added completely in the second edition:

> As therefore the highest perfection of intellectual nature lies in a careful and constant pursuit of true and solid happiness; so the care of ourselves, that we mistake not imaginary for real happi-

ness, is the necessary foundation of our *liberty*. The stronger ties we have to an unalterable pursuit of happiness in general, which is our greatest good, and which, as such, our desires always follow, the more are we free from any necessary determination of our *will* to any particular action, and from a necessary compliance with our desire, set upon any particular, and then appearing preferable good, till we have duly examin'd, whether it has a tendency to, or be inconsistent with, our real happiness; and therefore, till we are as much inform'd upon this enquiry as the weight of the matter, and the nature of the case demands, we are, by the necessity of prefering and pursuing true happiness as our greatest good, obliged to suspend the satisfaction of our desire in particular cases. (II.XXI.51)

Locke makes a claim in this passage about the nature of the "necessary foundation of our *liberty*." The "necessary foundation of our *liberty*" just is the Elusive Something: it is that which we need, over and above freedom of action, if our freedom of action is to count as liberty "worth the Name." He also tells us what it is in which the Elusive Something consists: it consists in stronger "ties" to an "unalterable pursuit of happiness in general." Now, I take it that to unalterably pursue "happiness in general" is to choose the right action—the action most conducive to happiness—whatever that action might be. It is not only to choose the good, but to track the good, to be "tied" to the good no matter where it lies. Further, Locke claims that when we do track the good in this manner, we are "free from any necessary determination of our *will* to any particular action." Notice that the talk here is of the actions of our wills—that is, he is talking of our volitions—and he is claiming that such actions are not necessarily determined "to any particular action" when we have such strong ties to an unalterable pursuit of happiness in general. To be *necessarily* determined is to be unfree— Locke is quite clear that freedom is opposed to necessity (cf. II.XXI.8–9)—so Locke is claiming that we are free with respect to particular acts of will when we are such that we track the good in our volitions. The kind of freedom being invoked cannot be freedom of action, for the question of whether or not we possess freedom of action is independent of any fact about the determination of volition. Hence, Locke must be asserting that to have one's volitions tied to the good—determined by the good—is to have another kind of freedom. What kind of freedom could it be? Only freedom of will, only, that is, the Elusive Something.

In addition, in order to maintain our ties to the pursuit of happiness in general—in order to track the good in our volitions—we are obliged on occasion to suspend the effect of uneasiness and deliberate. The exercise of our freedom to deliberate (our freedom of action with respect to deliberation) is required sometimes in order to have the right volitions, but it is not itself the "foundation of our *liberty*" except insofar as it is, sometimes, the only way to maintain our strong ties to the good; the suspension of desire followed by deliberation is, on occasion, the only way for an agent to bring it about that her volitions are determined by the good. But it is the having of such strong ties that is the "foundation of our *liberty*": it is what there is to liberty, true liberty, beyond freedom of action; it is the Elusive Something, it is freedom of will.

One sense of "necessity" is simply absence of freedom, and that is the sense that Locke invokes when he claims that our volitions are not necessary when they are determined by the good. (In fact, this is Locke's official definition of the term.) However, the sense of the term "necessity" in which it is contrasted with freedom is significantly different from the sense of "necessity" in which it refers to a modal notion such as logical or causal necessity. We have seen the former usage of the notion of necessity in the passage that I just quoted and discussed, the passage from II.XXI.51. But, interestingly, in the very next section, Locke invokes a modal notion of necessity. He says, in a passage quoted, in part, already:

> Whatever necessity determines to the pursuit of real Bliss, the same necessity, with the same force, establishes *suspence, deliberation*, and scrutiny of each successive desire, whether the satisfaction of it does not interfere with our true happiness, and mislead us from it. This, as seems to me is the great privilege of finite intellectual Beings; and I desire it may be well consider'd, whether

the great inlet and exercise of all the *liberty* Men have, are capable of, or can be useful to them, and that whereon depends the turn of their actions, does not lie in this, that they can *suspend* their desires, and stop them from determining their *wills* to any action, till they have duly and fairly *examin'd* the good and evil of it, as far forth as the weight of the thing requires. (II.XXI.52)[35]

Locke is quite openly agnostic here as to the exact sense in which "*suspence*" and "*deliberation*" are necessary. He leaves it open as to whether such actions are logically necessary, or logically necessary given God's plans, or causally necessary or what have you. These various senses of necessity may or may not be the particular sorts Locke had in mind, but it is not of importance exactly what senses he had in mind, for his point is only that no matter what the modal sense of the term "necessary" in which the actions of an agent who is "determine[d] to the pursuit of real Bliss" are necessary, the actions of suspending and deliberating are necessary in the same sense. Locke's point in equating the "necessity" through which deliberation occurs with the necessity of "pursui[ng] real Bliss" is significant: no one, he thinks, could object to having her volitions determined by "real Bliss"—no one would have reason to complain of her condition if her volitions track the good—and so no one could possibly object to the fact that she is necessitated to deliberate (however we specify this modal notion), for in deliberation she gets closer to the kind of determination of volition that we are after, the kind of determination in which the Elusive Something consists and which we mistakenly call freedom of will.

Both the "Second Try" and the "First Try" make the same mistake. The "First Try" goes wrong by identifying the capacities that are required to bring about perfection in the determination of volition with the perfection itself. Similarly, the "Second Try" goes wrong by identifying an accidental result of the exercise of such capacities—namely, accordance between volition and judgment—with the perfection itself. Locke cares about both the capacities for suspension and deliberation and the accordance between judgment and volition that can be achieved through their exercise precisely because he thinks that when all goes well, the exercise of such capacities and the resultant accordance that they issue in results in determination of volition by the good itself.

Something very close to the form of necessity that an agent is under when she is "determine[d] to the pursuit of real Bliss" is, I believe, very close to the notion of "moral necessity" popular in early modern philosophy. That is, many early modern thinkers used the term "moral necessity" to refer to the causal necessitation of an action or a choice by certain beliefs, judgments, or other psychic elements involved in the recognition of goodness. Descartes, for instance, refers to the determination of choice by a clear and distinct perception of the good as an example of "moral necessity."[36] Various early modern thinkers—including Descartes—insisted that such necessity was not opposed to freedom but could coexist with it.[37] Leibniz, for one, makes this point repeatedly. Consider, for instance, the following remark from his correspondence with Samuel Clarke:

> As for moral necessity, this also does not derogate from liberty. For when a wise being, and especially God who has supreme wisdom, chooses what is best, he is not the less free upon that account; on the contrary, it is the most perfect liberty not to be hindered from acting in the best manner. And when any other chooses according to the most apparent and strongly inclining good, he imitates therein the liberty of a truly wise being, in proportion to his disposition.[38]

Locke says more than just that moral necessitation is compatible with freedom; he also asserts that such necessitation is the Elusive Something, it is (what we mistakenly call) freedom of will. And this passage from Leibniz shows shades of the very same idea: It is through the moral necessity of our choices that we come to imitate God; it is when our choices are determined by the good that we are full-fledged free agents.[39]

To recapitulate: Locke's basic idea is that there is a relation that an agent can bear to an action that is properly called "freedom" (which I am calling "freedom of action"), but there are also various capacities without which an agent who has freedom of action lacks anything worth calling freedom at all, for she is not a full-fledged free agent. These capacities make up what I am calling the Elusive Something. Locke gives an account in the second and later editions of the nature of the Elusive Something under which an agent has it when either her volitions are determined by the good or she can bring it about that they are so determined, that is, she can bring her will within "the Sphere of . . . activity" of the good. In places, he refers to an agent who possesses this second perfection, who possesses the Elusive Something, as possessing what we mistakenly call freedom of will. The sense, however, in which the Elusive Something, the second perfection, is a kind of freedom at all is only an imprecise sense, for precisely speaking, the term "freedom" refers only to freedom of action.

Some Consequences of the Second Edition Account

Locke's settled view of the nature of (what we mistakenly call) freedom of will, his view of the nature of the Elusive Something, bears an interesting relationship to views under which freedom of will is what an agent had when she could have chosen differently than she did. Locke rejects the claim that freedom of will consists in openness or lack of determination in choice, but he agrees that *some* kind of openness (loosely conceived) is important. As we need to be good-tracking in our volitions, it needs to be the case that the best choice was not just the one we made, but was "open" to us in the following sense: had a different choice from the one we made been the right one, we would have made it instead. In a sense, Locke asks what the attraction is of the availability of alternative choices, and concludes that such availability is attractive only insofar as some alternative choice either was or might have turned out to be the best one. As freedom is a perfection, it is a part of the best human life, it must be worth having, and so it cannot be missing from an agent who lacks the ability to choose to "draw Shame and Misery upon" herself (II.XXI.50).

If Locke held the view of (what we mistakenly call) freedom of will captured in the "Third Try," then we can now see why it is that he overlooked Ayers's objection to the "First Try" account. We can put the Ayers objection in the form of a pointed question: If we need to be able to deliberate in order to have freedom of will with respect to an action, why don't we need to be able to deliberate about whether or not to deliberate, and, in turn, deliberate about whether or not to deliberate about whether or not to deliberate, and so on? The answer is that we need deliberation only insofar as through it we can bring it about that our volitions are determined by the good. It is hard to think of a circumstance in which we would need to deliberate about whether or not to deliberate—much less deliberate at one level deeper—in order to bring this about. If we could—as I suspect we could—construct such an example, this would show that sometimes, in order to have (what we mistakenly call) freedom of will, we need to deliberate about whether or not to deliberate. But given the rarity (and likely absurdity) of such examples, Locke felt no need to consider them. What I am suggesting, then, is that the reason that Locke overlooked the Ayers objection, despite the fact that he himself had offered a structurally identical objection, is that the Ayers objection is not an important objection to the view that he held; it is an important objection only to a view that he did not hold at all.

Notice that under the account of freedom of will, or the Elusive Something being attributed to Locke—what I am calling the "Third Try"—it is not enough to excuse an agent from blame for some action if some aspect of her circumstances or psychology causes her to have the wrong volition if that aspect of her condition does not also interfere with her freedom of action with respect to deliberation. For instance, if I offer you a small sum to embarrass yourself by dancing on the table (a sum not worth the embarrassment), and you greedily grab the money and embarrass yourself, you did not lack the Elusive Something (freedom of will under the account of the second edition), for there was nothing about my offer that would have prevented a choice on your part to deliberate from being efficacious. While my offer did bring about your choice to dance on the table (we can imagine), you still possessed freedom of action with respect to an action (deliberation) that would have been sufficient for allowing the good (the fact that dancing wasn't worth the money) to determine your choice. In such cases, agents do not lack freedom of will, for though their volitions are not determined by the good—were they so determined, such agents would not have done wrongly—they have the power to bring it about that their volitions are so determined. In such a case, the agent is guilty of a kind of negligence: had she exercised her freedom to deliberate (her freedom of action with respect to deliberation), she would have raised uneasinesses in herself in accordance with her judgments, and thereby have made the right choice. Locke puts the point like this:

> And here we may see how it comes to pass that a Man may justly incur punishment. . . . For though his *will* be always determined by that which is judged good by his Understanding, yet it excuses him not: Because, by a too hasty choice of his own making, he has imposed on himself wrong measures of good and evil. . . . If the neglect or abuse of the Liberty he had, to examine what would really and truly make for his Happiness, misleads him, the miscarriages that follow on it must be imputed to his own election. He had a Power to suspend his determination: It was given him, that he might examine, and take care of his own Happiness, and look that he were not deceived. (II.XXI.56)

It is by virtue of the fact that he has made "too hasty" a choice that an agent can be justly punished for wrongdoing. Such an agent has failed to exercise his freedom of action with respect to deliberation—his "Liberty . . . to examine what . . . make[s] for his Happiness"—and it is by virtue of this failure on his part that he can be justly punished.

Recall that Molyneux objects to Locke's first edition account on the grounds that under it, agents who chose and acted wrongly were to be held morally responsible in a large class of cases, despite the fact that their actions did not express that "depravity of will" that, Molyneux evidently thinks, is needed to justify such attributions. What this objection suggested was that Locke needed to produce a more nuanced set of distinctions among agents who have incorrect volitions than he had offered in the first edition. We have already seen some of the complexity that Locke added. In particular, Locke notes a distinction between two kinds of agents, both of whom have correct judgments, but choose wrongly: the first sort enjoy freedom of action with respect to deliberation, the second sort do not. The voluntary evil actions of agents of the second sort express depravity of will only in the weak sense in which they express a depraved volition, the volition by virtue of which the action is voluntary. The voluntary evil actions of agents of the first sort express depravity of will in that weak way, but also in another way: They indicate that the agent failed to bring it about that her volitions were determined by the good, despite the fact that it was in her power to do so, since she had freedom of action with respect to deliberation.

Locke draws another distinction between agents who choose wrongly that I have not yet mentioned. As the first distinction was a distinction between agents who choose wrongly even though they have correct judgments, the second distinction is a distinction between agents who choose wrongly and have mistaken judgments. In a passage added in the second edition, he says:

> Fashion and the common Opinion having settled wrong Notions, and education and custom ill habits, the just values of things are misplaced, and the palates of Men corrupted. Pains should be taken to rectify these; and contrary habits change our pleasures, and give a relish to that which is necessary or conducive to our Happiness. (II.XXI.69)

Here, Locke is discussing people who, as a result of "fashion," "common Opinion," "education," or "custom" have corrupted palates. What he has in mind are people who fail to take pleasure in things that are conducive to their long-term happiness. The passage follows a discussion of the various ways, through repeated trials, a person can come to habituate herself to something that is good for her. Locke sees such habituation as the only way through which a person who has developed the wrong tastes can come to have right volitions. The point I wish to highlight, however, is that Locke has identified, here, another distinction between agents who choose wrongly that was absent from the first edition. There is a distinction between two kinds of agents, both of whom choose wrongly out of mistaken judgments: there are those who make mistaken judgments out of sloth or negligence, who just fail to examine their circumstances closely enough and see which of their actions promise the greatest pleasure—Locke noted the possibility of agents of this sort in the first edition, as I have discussed above—and there are those who do not fail in this regard but who make mistaken judgments as a result of having corrupted palates brought on through poor education or other kinds of mishabituation. The wrong actions of agents of the latter sort are less expressive of "depravity of will" than are the wrong actions of agents of the former sort.[40]

In the second and later editions, then, Locke has accomplished two related tasks: he has offered an account of the nature of the Elusive Something, (what we mistakenly call) freedom of will, and he has used this account and the supporting account of the determination of volition to produce a richly textured picture of the differences and similarities between agents who act wrongly, a picture that Molyneux felt (and Locke agreed) was absent from the first edition.

FREEDOM OF WILL AND THE NATURAL LAW THEORY

There is a question, which I aim to address in this section, as to the degree to which Locke's view of the Elusive Something, as I have described it, is separable from various philosophical positions that Locke held, but which contemporary philosophers tend to eschew. In particular, there are a number of aspects of Locke's natural law theory that we might wish to reject. The first concern is epistemological: If our freedom turns on the degree to which our volitions are determined by the good, then our freedom seems to rest, in part, on our capacity to know what is, actually, good. But are there resources within a natural law theory like Locke's to describe nonsupernatural mechanisms through which we can come to know what is and is not good? The second concern is metaphysical: Can we accept

Locke's view of the Elusive Something without accepting a strong form of realism about value of the kind that Locke espoused?

Locke thinks that we can determine through reason which actions are right and wrong by examining the causal sequences that follow from those actions. The action that results in the greatest personal pleasure, taking into consideration one's standing in the afterlife, is the right action to perform. In order to bring it about that our volitions are determined by the good, we need to reason carefully and make future goods alive to ourselves by raising appropriate present uneasiness in their absence.[41] As a result of this view, Locke thinks that a feature of an agent's circumstances or psychology undermines her freedom of will just in case it has two effects on her condition: it causes her volition to be determined by something other than the good, and it detracts from her freedom of action with respect to deliberation.[42]

If we accept that the right action is that action which accords with natural law, and accept that God has brought about accord between those actions and the actions that maximize the agent's personal pleasure, accurate reasoning about which action will maximize my personal pleasure requires at the very least that my reasoning is guided by some form of awareness of God's laws. If the action that I settle upon is in violation of God's law, then I will suffer punishment in the afterlife, but if it is not, then I will not; so, I cannot determine which of my possible actions is going to maximize my pleasure without already knowing what God's laws are. Certainly, however, I cannot come to know God's laws solely through causal reasoning and calculations of the various pleasures and pains that I will feel. So, Locke needs a story as to how it is that we come to know God's laws independent of causal calculation of the various pleasures and pains that will follow from our conduct. Although Locke probably thought that we usually come to know God's laws through revelation (more on this in a moment), it is not at all obvious that human beings, under Locke's account of their nature, have at their disposal *non*supernatural means to come to know God's laws.

Locke does say, repeatedly, that morality, like mathematics, is "capable of demonstration" (cf. I.III.1, III.XI.16, IV.III.18, IV.XII.8). This view is a consequence of Locke's view that moral concepts, like mathematical concepts and unlike ideas of substances, are constructed voluntarily by the mind. He holds that through introspection we can uncover the entire structure in simple ideas of moral concepts, and, thereby, discover relationships between them. He thinks, for instance, that the claim that murder is wrong is a consequence of the concepts of murder and the concept of wrong, just as the claim that $2 + 3 = 5$ is a consequence of the concepts of two, three, plus, equals, and five. Further, determining which actions are murders (and which are, say, mercy killings) is a matter of examining the ideas that we have of each action and seeing whether or not they fall under the idea of murder. And Locke does seem to think that we know natural law, or at least have the obligation to know it, because morality is capable of demonstration (cf. I.III.2). Especially given Locke's rejection of the innateness of moral principles, it seems peculiar that we should be able to determine the content of *God's* laws through examination of *our* concepts. But, even if we look past this peculiarity, all of this only shows that, if Locke is right, we can determine the content of God's laws if we have all the relevant concepts and if we are sophisticated reasoners, if we are capable of being mathematicians of moral concepts.[43] That is, to know God's laws we will have to be furnished with all the concepts from which the laws can be derived, and we must be capable of performing the requisite derivations. Insofar as the concepts from which the laws are derivable might include simple ideas to which we have not had exposure—either through sensation or reflection—we might be genuinely unable to perform the derivations without first gaining exposure to the requisite simple ideas. In short, there are a variety of reasons for thinking that even if it is a fact, which it might not be, that "morality is capable of demonstration," we might still be unable to determine the content of God's laws.

We can certainly imagine other nonsupernatural means by which we would come to know the content of God's laws, although some such means—such as the innateness of moral principles—are not Lockean in spirit. Locke, then, has an optimistic picture of what human beings are capable of in deliberation. From this optimism arises his view that just those aspects of our circumstances or psychology that eliminate our freedom of action with respect to deliberation are also those that interfere with our ability to bring it about that our volitions are determined by the good. Locke thinks that we can, at least sometimes, really come to know the nature of God's laws, and thereby determine which of our actions promises the most pleasure and the least pain (in the long run), and then make those future pleasures and pains alive for ourselves in the form of uneasinesses. However, Locke claims explicitly that his optimism in this regard is not predicated upon a belief in the power of the natural faculties exercised in deliberation, but rather upon his belief in divine providence. God will give us what we need to know the good, Locke thinks. He will give us what we need by first investing us with natural faculties, but going on to make up for what we lack the sagacity to know through their exercise by providing us with revelation. For instance, in *The Reasonableness of Christianity*, Locke says:

> It should seem, by the little that has hitherto been done in it, that it is too hard a task for unassisted reason to establish morality in all its parts, upon its true foundations, with a clear and convincing light. And it is at least a surer and shorter way, to the apprehensions of the vulgar, and mass of mankind, that one manifestly sent from God, and coming with visible authority from him, should, as a king and lawmaker, tell them their duties and require their obedience, than leave it to the long and sometime intricate deductions of reason, to be made out by them. Such trains of reasoning the greatest part of mankind have neither leisure to weigh, nor, for want of education and use, skill to judge of.[44]

While revelation might not be indispensable in principle, it is indispensable in fact. We need God's help if we are to come to know the demonstrable moral truths. But if we don't wish to accept on faith the claim that God will provide us with just what we need in order to know the good, then mere freedom of action with respect to deliberation will not guarantee (not even necessarily guarantee "for all practical purposes") that we are able to bring it about that our volitions are determined by the good. Locke's optimism, then, is not founded upon a belief in the efficacy of some nonsupernatural mechanism through which we come to know the good, but rather, on a belief in the reliability of revelation. And, further, the prospects for a satisfying nonsupernatural account of such mechanisms, within Locke's natural law theory, appear quite dim.

What follows from this is that if Locke's view of freedom of will as determination of volition by the good (or the power to arrange such determination) is to be cleaved from his theological commitments, we must furnish something that Locke does not provide: an account of the nature and source of the evaluative facts under which they are knowable by us through nonsupernatural means. It is open to Locke to respond that his is a theory of the nature of freedom, not its extent. Thus, if knowledge of the good is required for freedom and difficult to gain, all this shows is that freedom is rare, not that his account of its nature is mistaken. But I don't think this is the right response to make on Locke's behalf. Rather, it is worth scrutinizing the claim that his view of freedom really requires the kind of knowledge of the evaluative facts that seems difficult to provide within a natural law theory. In particular, Locke's theory of freedom seems to require not knowledge *that*, but knowledge *how*. That is, if our volitions are to depend upon, or track, the good, we need to be invested with dispositions that result in different volitions, depending on where the good lies. To be invested with such dispositions is to possess a *kind* of knowledge, but the kind of knowledge that is involved here might not include an ability to articulate or to describe what it is that is good about the best of one's alternative actions. It might not even involve a disposition to assent to articulations of true evaluative claims of certain sorts after careful consideration; the possession of such dispositions needn't involve any strictly *intellectual* capacities at all. To put the point in Locke's terms, the capacity for tracking the good needn't involve the capacity to gain any *ideas* of the good, as good, at all. All such a capacity need involve is a tendency to aversion—uneasiness—with the prospect of wrong action and a tendency to attraction to—uneasiness in the want of—right action. Since any satisfying theory of the source of value properties will have to be such as to allow for the genuine possibility that agents can be disposed to act in a way appropriate to the evaluative facts, the failures of Locke's natural law theory with respect to the prospects for knowledge of value properties do not speak against the strength of his position with regard to freedom. Locke does think of determination of volition by the good as resting on knowledge of natural law, knowledge that is usually obtained only through supernatural means. But there is nothing about his theory of freedom that strictly requires this view.

Locke's natural law theory is a form of value realism: under the theory, the evaluative facts are a function of features of the world that are independent of the sentiments, acts, or attitudes of any set of actual or hypothetical agents. Depending on one's stance toward the issue of the ontological status of value, this can seem either an advantage or a detriment of his view. However, the kind of value realism that is implied by Locke's natural law theory is not required for the credibility of his view of the Elusive Something. It is true that if some very strong forms of egoism about value are true, then Locke's theory of freedom of will becomes indistinguishable from weaker, and less interesting, views. The most extreme example of this can be seen by considering what is left over of Locke's view if what is best for a particular agent to do is just what that agent wants most to do. If this extreme kind of egoism about value were true, then an agent whose volition is determined by the good is just an agent whose volition is determined by what she most wants. Such a position is equivalent in all essential respects to the kind of deflationary compatibilism espoused by Hobbes. In fact, to put the point in the language of the introduction to this book, if what is best for an agent to do is merely a function of facts about that agent herself, then Locke's self-transcendence theory is merely a kind of self-expression theory: An agent has freedom of will just in case those aspects of herself that are constitutive of the good are expressed in her volition.

But, surely, egoistic theories of value are, in all their forms, false. What is best, or right, or good is simply not a function of any one person's attitude, or opinion. This is just to say that at the very least, value properties have some intersubjective status. Further, this is all that is required for Locke's view of freedom of will to be distinctively different from any self-expression theory. So long as determination of volition by the good means dependency of one's volition on features of the world that are constituted by facts external to oneself, self-transcendence theories remain importantly different from any kind of self-expression view. Notice that Locke's natural law theory, then, in implying a strong form of value realism, implies more than Locke's view of freedom of will requires in order to have its distinctive character. In implying that value properties are a function of natural law, Locke's theory does imply that value properties are intersubjective properties; in fact, it implies something stronger: Value properties are not only not fixed by any *one* individual's states, acts, dispositions, or attitudes— which is all that is required for them to have an intersubjective status—they are not fixed by the states, acts, dispositions, or attitudes of *any* individual persons or hypothetical persons. It is therefore open to those who are attracted to Locke's theory of freedom of will to accept a theory of value that shares the weaker implication of his natural law theory and departs from the stronger.

Thus, the two most important features of Locke's natural law theory that many, although not all, contemporary philosophers will want to reject—that the most realistic chance for knowledge of the good is only through supernatural mechanisms, and that value properties are not even in part a function of particular contingent facts about actual or hypothetical agents—can be rejected without rejection of Locke's self-transcendence theory of freedom of will.

CONCLUSION

One way to approach the problem of free agency—an approach that is common in contemporary philosophy—begins with the thought that freedom is necessary for moral responsibility. To test an account of the nature of free agency, when approaching the issue from this point of view, we try to see whether or not moral distinctions that we want to draw between agents correspond appropriately to the distinctions in freedom implied by the account being tested. We ask, for instance, whether an agent who is unfree according to the account being tested is appropriately excused from blame for wrong action. As I suggested in the introduction, there is another way in which we might approach the problem of free agency. We might begin not by trying to understand the necessary conditions of moral responsibility, but rather by trying to understand the nature of divine agency, or, in secular terms, ideal agency. If this is our approach, then we will test an account of the nature of free agency by, for instance, asking the following question: Is an agent who is free according to the account being tested exemplative of agency-at-its-best? If, as in Locke's account, the full-fledged free agent enjoys (or has the power to bring about) determination of volition by the good, then in testing the account we might ask the following questions: Why would we have any interest in having our volitions determined in any other way? But if we do not have any interest in having our volitions determined in any other way, then how could we be more perfect, how could we approach the appearance of God, by lacking such determination? As is evident from a passage already quoted, it is this latter approach that Locke takes:

> Is it worth the Name of *Freedom* to be at liberty to play the Fool and draw Shame and Misery upon a Man's self? If to break loose from the conduct of Reason, and to want that restraint of Examination and Judgment, which keeps us from chusing or doing the worse, be *Liberty*, true Liberty, mad Men and Fools are the only Freemen: But yet, I think, nobody would chuse to be mad for the sake of such *Liberty*, but he that is mad already. (II.XXI.50; II.XXI.32, first edition)

In Locke's second edition account, then, freedom of will is something that an agent possesses when she embodies an ideal of agency, when she exemplifies agency-at-its-best; freedom of will, that is, is a perfection. Locke thinks that the best sort of determination of volition is determination of volition by the good—this is the kind of determination of volition enjoyed by God and angels (cf. II.XXI.49, quoted earlier)—and it is because such determination of volition is the best sort that the agent who possesses it possesses freedom of will. To understand the nature of freedom of will is to understand the most important sense in which our agency is like divine agency: the will of a full-fledged free agent, like the will of God, is guided inexorably by the good.

The passage just discussed provides another reason for rejecting the interpretation offered in the "Second Try." Why would it be a perfection for one's volitions to be determined in accordance with one's judgments? Perhaps there is something good about such determination—perhaps, for instance, lack of conflict in one's psyche is of intrinsic merit—but Locke never shows any inclination to suggest that there is anything valuable about accordance between volition and judgment *except* when one's judgments are accurate. However, the kind of perfection that we instantiate when our volitions come about in accordance with judgments that are themselves determined by the good is a perfection achievable by having volitions that are determined by the good without the aid of judgments.

In the introduction, I suggested that in Locke's account of the nature of free agency, freedom is not to be equated with the highest form of self-expressive agency. We are now in a better position to see what that claim amounts to. The conduct of an agent who enjoys freedom of action depends on something about her, and is, in that sense, to some degree self-expressive. Her actions are not merely at the whim of circumstance; her conduct depends—not entirely, but partially—on herself, on her will. The project of understanding how an agent can be the source of her conduct is the project of understanding the various ways in which an agent's conduct can depend on her, and understanding the various ways her conduct must depend on her if she is to be morally responsible for it. An agent who has freedom of action expresses herself in her conduct, for she stands—or, at least, something about her stands—in a crucial position in the causal etiology of her actions. Locke's account of freedom of action is his attempt to describe both necessary and sufficient conditions for the kind and degree of dependency of conduct on oneself that human beings should hope, and can expect, to possess.[45]

But, as I suggested in the introduction, there is another aspect of full-fledged free agency that we cannot hope to capture in an account of self-expressive agency. The full-fledged free agent doesn't just express herself in her conduct, she also transcends herself; she transcends herself through the attainment of an ideal of agency. It is Locke's account of (what we mistakenly call) freedom of will that is intended to capture this aspect of free agency. The full-fledged free agent has both freedom of action—she expresses herself in her conduct—and freedom of will—she transcends and escapes herself and thereby becomes like God.

It is a mistake to be a Hobbesean. It is a mistake, that is, to simply dismiss the intuitions that many of us feel that there is more to full-fledged free agency than freedom of action. It is a mistake also—as I hope has become clear—to read Locke as just another Hobbesean. Locke's view of free agency is distinctive precisely by virtue of what he *adds* to Hobbes's view. Locke recognized that free agency is dual: it consists of not just one perfection in the determination of action, but two. We are free agents not just because we are able to avoid the obstacles to success in action that the world throws at us, but also because we are the sorts of creatures that respond to value in the world; we are the sorts of creatures whose choices can be formed by those aspects of the world that really matter, those aspects that are truly good. And when our choices are formed in this way, our conduct expresses something better than it would if it merely expressed ourselves.

2

Volition and Voluntary Action

THE PROBLEM of agency—in the form in which we usually think of it—is the problem of discovering a metaphysical basis for an intuitive distinction: the difference between happenings and doings. Judgments of moral responsibility depend crucially on this distinction—doings are, and happenings are not, the kinds of occurrences about which such judgments are justified. If we can't find a metaphysical basis for the distinction, moral judgments may seem to be based on little more than a metaphor, a difference that we recognize but which eludes the kind of justification that moral judgments demand. If we think of mere happenings—events that do not reveal the presence of any agency whatsoever—as the basic events that there are, if we accept this common naturalistic assumption, then the problem of agency becomes a problem of reduction: How can we take a group of mere happenings and add them together to create an action? Actions, after all, have a flavor to them that happenings do not: The rock skips across the water, and the child skips along the sidewalk, but the child's skipping expresses something about the child—belongs, we might say, to the child—in a way that the rock's skipping does not belong to it. Our awareness and employment of this distinction emerge in the varying attitudes that we might take toward the child or the rock: while we might praise the child for her lithe skipping, we would praise the person who threw the rock, and not the rock itself, for its skipping. Actions are traceable to their performers; happenings are no more parts of the things that they are happening to than they are parts of any wider chunk of the world that includes them. How can the distinctive aspect of action be found in a compilation of bare, inert occurrences?

The problem of agency arises out of the recognition that there are differences in strength or depth or richness in attributability of events to objects. To be sure, we attribute the skipping to the rock: we call it "the rock's skipping," but in attributing the skipping to the child, we seem to be engaging in a different kind of attribution. What is this different kind of attributability? It is tempting to reach for the difference with woefully vague terms: To attribute to a *person* is to specify a relation that is "stronger" or "deeper" or "richer" than the relation specified when attributing a property to an object. But in calling the difference that we recognize a difference in "strength" or "depth" or "richness," we only manage to express a feeling that there is a difference—we get no closer to identifying the nature of that difference. We want to find a basis for this intuitive difference in attributability. What is it about our actions that accounts for the fact that they are attributable to us in the strong, deep, rich way definitive of agency, of personhood?

In a certain respect, it might seem anachronistic to look to early modern philosophy for an answer to this question. After all, it is relatively recently that the problem of agency has been made explicit as a problem. Early modern philosophers did often use a distinction between action and passion. (This is explicit in Descartes, Spinoza, Locke, Leibniz, Hume, and Reid, to name a few.) This distinction was an offshoot of the Aristotelian distinction between action and passion—a distinction intended to characterize the difference between those substances that receive changes and those that impart them—and doesn't seem, at first glance at least, to have much to do with the distinction between happenings and doings; it doesn't seem to have much to do with different modes of attributability. In a sense, this is correct: The distinction between action and passion is not the distinction between doings and happenings. However, as I argue for Locke's case, the distinction between action and passion is relevant to the problem of agency, for in it we find a basis for *a* difference in attributability; while it is not the difference in attributability that we are ultimately after—it is not, that is, the basis for the distinction between happenings and doings—it is, nevertheless, a first step toward understanding the kind of deep attributability typical of full-fledged agency.

The relevance of Locke's distinction between action and passion comes from the fact that genuine doings are none of them passions; that is, we need the distinction between action and passion to identify the class of states and events that are even potentially full-fledged doings. But the distinction does not do all the work that needs to be done, since genuine doings are a proper subset of those states and events that are not passions. Understanding Locke's distinction between action and passion, then, is only the first step toward understanding his contribution to the problem of agency. However, the real progress that Locke made was in his account of volition and its role in voluntary action. Locke's distinction between voluntary and involuntary actions—a distinction among those states and events that are not passions—is very close to the distinction between doings and happenings, the distinction that we are ultimately after when we think about the problem of agency.

The purpose of this chapter is, first, to tease a metaphysics of agency from Locke's texts—for it is in this metaphysics that the distinction between voluntary and involuntary action emerges—and, second, to explicate the contribution of this metaphysics to the problem of agency. I argue, first, that for Locke there is a distinction in degree of attributability of modifications to substances that, while not sufficient for accounting for the kind of strong attributability that we think of as central to full-fledged agency, is one step toward accounting for it. This distinction is captured in the distinction between passion and (what I call) proper action. Proper actions are more strongly attributable to substances than passions, for proper actions express not just the presence in the substance of the power to produce the modification (as is also true of passions), but also the power to produce the cause of the modification. In Locke's view, there is another set of actions that are attributable to sub-

stances in a stronger way yet: proper actions that satisfy, and
are (therefore) brought about by volitions. Locke calls these
"voluntary actions." Voluntary actions, unlike other proper actions, are attributable to persons, and never to mere substances,
because the mental act of volition is constituted in part by an
act of self-conscious awareness of the kind that Locke takes to
be constitutive of personal identity. Our voluntary actions *belong* to us because they bear an intimate relationship to a state
that lies within the boundary of the person, a boundary that is
constituted by an act of self-conscious awareness.

Locke's metaphysics of agency is of relevance, also, for understanding Locke's account of what I have called in chapter 1
freedom of action. That is, Locke thinks that we have freedom
of action with respect to a particular action when we have both
the power to voluntarily perform the action and the power to
voluntarily refrain from the action. But this account remains
obscure without clear criteria that an agent must satisfy if she
is to have each of these powers. Providing clear criteria requires
articulating the necessary and sufficient conditions for possession of a power of any sort, and necessary and sufficient conditions for voluntary action. (Voluntary refraining is, as I argued
in chapter 1, merely a special case of voluntary action.) The
results of this chapter can be used to provide these analyses.

ACTION AND ACTIVE POWERS

It is often asserted that Locke (and many of his contemporaries)
held a volitional theory of action. A volitional theory of action
is any theory that says that an event or state (mental or physical)
counts as an action, as something done, by virtue of its relationship to a volition on the part of the agent.[1] As I will argue in
later sections, this is, in fact, more true than not: When we use
the term "action" to mean a genuine doing, then it is true that
Locke holds a volitional theory of action, for those modifications of substances that are attributable in the special sense that
we are trying to capture, those that are closest to being full-
fledged doings, are so by virtue of their relationship to volitions.

However, Locke did not use the term "action" in this way; many events and states that Locke would call "actions" bear no relationship at all to any volition on the part of any agent. Further, many states and events that fall under Locke's term "action"—as he officially defines it—are not doings at all. In short, Locke neither uses nor defines the term "action" by appeal to volition, nor does he intend his definition (nor does it serve) as an account of the distinction between happenings and doings. Nevertheless, as I argue in this section, Locke did use the term "actions" to identify a set of modifications of substances that are more strongly attributable to those substances than mere "passions," and, hence, Locke's distinction between action and passion does make one small step toward a solution to the problem of agency.

Passion and Proper Action

Locke takes his systematic account of action (offered in one of the last sections of II.XXI and absent completely from the *Essay* prior to the fourth edition) to be cleaning up some of the messiness in the way in which the term was thrown about in ordinary discourse. He says:

> [I]t may perhaps be to our purpose, and help to give us clearer conceptions about *power*, if we make our thoughts take a little more exact survey of *Action*. I have said above, that we have *Ideas* but of two sorts of *Action*, viz. *Motion* and *Thinking*. These, in truth, though called and counted *Actions*, yet, if nearly considered, will not be found to be always perfectly so. For, if I mistake not, there are instances of both kinds, which, upon due consideration, will be found rather *Passions* than *Actions*. (II.XXI.72)

That category of states and events that are "called and counted" actions are not all of them really actions in the sense that Locke is defining. Let's call the set of things that are "called and counted" actions "actions," and the subset of those that are *properly* called actions "proper actions." Those actions that are not proper actions are called "passions."[2] This taxonomy is important, for most of the time that Locke uses the term "action," he is referring to a member of the broad class of actions rather than particularly picking out a member of the subclass of proper actions; thus, he often uses the term "action" to apply equally to passions and proper actions. This is just to say that Locke himself tends to use the term "action" in the casual way that he thinks imprecise.

Later in the same section, Locke offers his substantive account of the nature of actions, proper actions, and passions. He says:

> Whatsoever modification a substance has, whereby it produces any effect, that is called *Action*: *v.g.* a solid substance, by motion, operates on or alters the sensible *Ideas* of another substance, and therefore this modification of motion we call Action. But yet this motion in that solid substance is, when rightly considered, but a passion, if it received it only from some external Agent. So that the *Active Power* of motion is in no substance which cannot begin motion in itself or in another substance when at rest. So likewise in *Thinking*, a Power to receive *Ideas* or Thoughts, from the operation of any external substance, is called a *Power* of thinking: but this is but a *Passive Power*, or Capacity. But to be able to bring into view *Ideas* out of sight at one's own choice, and to compare which of them one thinks fit, this is an *Active Power*. (II.XXI.72)

Locke seems to think that the term "action"—used in the broad sense in which "proper actions" are a subset of "actions"—is used to pick out a modification of a substance as a cause in a cause-effect transaction. That is, he seems to think that we call a modification of a substance an "action" (in the broad sense) when we take it to be the cause of some other modification; to call a modification of a substance an "action" in this sense is merely to say that it is a cause of some effect.[3] Any modification of a substance is (potentially at least) an "action" in this broad sense, for any modification of a substance might be taken to be the cause of some effect. But this usage of the term "action" fails to identify the attribute of modifications that is of metaphysical import, since there are "actions" in this sense that are proper actions and others that are passions. So, Locke offers an account of the distinction between proper actions and passions. A passion is a modification of a substance S that is caused *solely* by modifications of things external to S: an object's motion is "but a passion" if "it received it only from some external Agent." A proper action of S is a modification of S that is caused (at least in part) by some modification of S itself:[4] to consider a particular idea "at one's own choice"—that is, as a result of a modification internal to the mind doing the considering—is to engage in a proper action.[5] For instance, the wax melts as a result of exposure to the sun. The melting of the wax is a passion of the wax (rather than a proper action), for it is caused by a modification of the sun (namely, the heat of the sun), and not by a modification of the wax itself. However, imagine that a muscle spasm in me (caused, say, by an electric shock) causes my hand to rise. The movement of my hand is a proper action of mine, for it is caused by a modification of me: my muscle spasm. The muscle spasm, however, is a passion of mine, for it is caused by a modification of, say, a car battery.

Some readers might be bothered by the fact that I place no emphasis on Locke's usage of the word "begin" in the passage just quoted. Locke does say that "the *Active Power* of motion is in no substance which cannot begin motion in itself or in another substance," and it is also the case that under my interpretation of the passage, a substance's motion is going to count as a proper action of the substance just in case it is caused by a modification of the same substance. It might be claimed that an object can move, and the movement can be caused by one of its own modifications (as in a windup toy) without the object *beginning* its own motion; in the case of the windup toy, the motion is begun by a turning of the key. As we can always stretch our causal chains one step further back in time (what caused the key to turn?), this line of thought pushes toward a substance-causal reading of Locke's account of action: A motion is begun by a substance just in case the motion, or the modification of the substance by virtue of which the motion is caused, is caused by the substance itself and not by any modification of the substance. While there are other passages that push toward this interpretation (cf. II.XXI.29, but see also my discussion of this passage in chapter 3), they are far from definitive. Further, there is a natural interpretation of what it means to "begin" a motion under which there is no need to interpret Locke as holding a substance-causal view: for a substance to begin a particular motion, a modification of the substance must cause the motion to begin. Hence, when Locke says that a substance must begin motion in itself (or another substance) in order to have the active power of motion, he may very well mean only that the motion must be caused by a modification of the substance.

There are lots of modifications of ourselves that are proper actions in Locke's sense but which we do not think of as things that we do at all; we think of them as happenings rather than doings. The example of the electricity-induced muscle spasm that causes my arm to rise illustrates the point. Modern theories of action have tried to avoid classifying cases of this sort as action at all. This should come, however, as no surprise: Locke is offering his version of the Aristotelian distinction between passion and action, a distinction intended to pick out an important feature of causal interactions in general and not an important feature of, particularly, causal transactions involving agents.

This much, then, is clear: The distinction between passion and proper action does not draw the line between doings and happenings. However, this does not mean that the distinction is not relevant to the problem of agency. But what relevance does the distinction have to agency? To answer this question, I must first describe Locke's account of active and passive powers and their relationship to passions and proper actions.

Active and Passive Power

Powers, for Locke—as Michael Ayers has emphasized[6]—are placeholders in our understanding. That is, they are necessarily presupposed by our causal explanations, but we do not know their exact nature. Whenever we say that one state or change caused another, we presuppose that there is an active power in the subject of the first to cause such states or changes in the second, and there is a passive power in the subject of the second to receive such states or changes. As Locke puts the point:

> [W]hatever Change is observed, the Mind must collect a Power somewhere, able to make that Change, as well as a possibility in the thing it self to receive it. (II.XXI.4)

To "collect a Power" in an object is to ascribe a power to the object, and Locke seems to think that to do so is to fill in a conceptual gap in any causal explanation. A fully satisfying explanation of any event—the sort of explanation that the corpuscularian science was supposed to provide—would articulate the nature of the powers of objects. That is, such an explanation would show what it was about the object in which the event occurred, and what it was about the objects that triggered the event, that made it the case that the event occurred. To invoke a power—as we do at least implicitly in any explanation that fails to be a complete explanation—is to indicate that there was something about the object to which the power is ascribed by virtue of which the object brought about or received a particular state or change, but it is not to say precisely what it was about the object that accounted for the occurrence. Powers are the we-know-not-what in objects by virtue of which objects cause changes in other objects and have changes caused in themselves. We might even say that powers fill the conceptual gap between cause and effect that is left when we conceive of no more than a constant conjunction between them.[7] To say, then, that a substance's modification (either a passion or a proper action of the substance) expresses the substance's power to A is to say that there is some underlying structure in the object, of whose nature we know virtually nothing, by virtue of which it causes or receives modifications of type A.[8]

Notice, then, that for Locke, it is both necessary and sufficient for a substance's possession of a power that some conditional is true of the substance. For instance, for the wax to have the power to be melted, it needs only be true that if the wax were to be in certain circumstances, it would melt. If this conditional is true of the wax, then the wax has a power to melt, and if the wax has the power to melt, then the conditional must be true of it. For the wax to have the power to melt at ninety-seven degrees, it must be the case that if the wax were at ninety-seven degrees, it would melt. Since a power to A is no more than that aspect of the object by virtue of which it engages in or produces modifications of type A (depending on whether the power is active or passive—more of this shortly), those substances that possess the power are all and only those of which some appropriate conditional is true.

Active and passive powers are distinguished by Locke in the following passage:

> Power thus considered is two-fold, viz. as able to make, or able to receive any change. The one may be called *Active*, and the other *Passive Power*. (II.XXI.2)

Passions are expressive of only passive powers of the substances in which they inhere or occur. This follows from the fact that if an object has a passion of type A, then that passion must have been (by definition) caused by a modification of another object (or set of objects), and hence we know (from consideration of the passion alone) that the object is able to receive changes of type A, but not necessarily able to produce them.

Proper actions, on the other hand, express active powers of the substances in which they inhere or occur. This follows from the definition of active power and the definition of proper action: If a modification of S (of type A) is a proper action, then it is a modification of S that was caused by another modification of S. Hence, S is capable of bringing about changes of type A and therefore has an active power to do so. Proper actions, however, are not the only means by which an active power can be expressed. The active power of an object can also be expressed by a change in another object entirely. So, the melting of the wax when placed in the sunlight expresses an active power to melt wax that belongs to the sun. (It also expresses a passive power of the wax to be melted.)

There is one consequence of Locke's view of powers—which Locke himself never seems to acknowledge—that is worthy of note, for it is not immediately obvious and it has important consequences for understanding his view: A particular power of a substance could count as *both* an active *and* a passive power; a particular power could count as an active power to produce one kind of modification and a passive power to engage in another kind of modification. Consider again the example of my electricity-induced muscle spasm that causes my arm to rise. I am—or, rather, my body is—rightly said to have a passive power with regard to muscle spasms, as there is some state of my body by virtue of which I received the muscle spasm; there is something about me, although we don't know what it is, by virtue of which I have muscle spasms when exposed to electric shocks (in certain circumstances). My body is also rightly said to have an active power to raise my arm, for the rising of my arm is a proper action: it is a modification of me caused by a modification of me. However, since the muscle spasm caused my arm to rise, it seems plausible that my passive power to have muscle spasms is also an active power to raise arms: it is the state of me, we-know-not-what, by virtue of which I am able to receive muscle spasms, and raise my arm (by having muscle spasms). In short, the very same state of a substance by virtue of which it endures one kind of modification might also be the state of the substance by virtue of which it produces another. This point will become important for understanding why it is that proper actions are more strongly attributable to substances than mere passions. (The point is also important for understanding Locke's account of volition described in detail a little later.)

Two Degrees of Attributability

We are now in a position to see the contribution to the problem of agency made by the distinction between passion and proper action: There is a stronger connection between a proper action and the substance in which it inheres than there is between a passion and the very same substance precisely because passions are expressive of passive powers and actions are expressive of active powers. This is not a sufficient explanation, however, without an account of why it is that the expression of active power ties the relevant action more closely to the substance than the expression of passive power. Here is a possible explanation:

Objects, like Descartes's wax, endure through changes in their states and through the occurrence and completion of events in which they figure. States and events (modifications) are fleeting things: frequently enough, they happen and they are gone. But we do not think of them as disappearing without a trace; rather, we think of substances as intimately tied to those earlier modifications well after they are gone. One way (although not the only way) to explain this is by appeal to the fact that modifications indicate the presence in substances of something enduring, something that continues to be part of the substance well after the modification is gone. Locke tells us what it is that endures: powers. That is, although the modification is started and completed, never to return—think of the texture of the wax—what endures is the potential for the substance to produce or endure a similar modification again; what endures is whatever it was about the substance by virtue of which the modification occurred in the first place. Active powers justify a stronger kind of attributability of modification than passive powers. When a substance A's (engages in a modification of type A), and thereby expresses its active power to A, it is not just the occurrence of A that has its trace in the substance in the form of the power, but also an occurrence of the modification that brought A about. Active powers are more deeply embedded in the substances that have them than passive powers are: active powers are what accounts for not just the occurrence of one particular modification of a substance, but also for the source of the occurrence of that modification. So, for instance, in the case of the muscle spasm that causes my arm to rise, the rising of my arm expresses two powers in me: a passive power to have my arm rise, and a passive power to have muscle spasms. The second of these powers is also an active power to raise my arm, as muscle spasms of the relevant sort cause my arm to rise. We find in the substance (me) a dual source of the modification (the rising of my arm). Proper actions, therefore, express more about the substance in which they inhere than any passion could, for a passion can only express a single passive power to have certain sorts of modifications.

To put the point another way: Any modification (whether a passion or a proper action) expresses *something* about the substance in which it inheres. That is, any modification expresses something about the nature of the relevant substance. But more is expressed about the nature of a substance by a proper action than is expressed by a passion, for two aspects of the substance's nature are expressed by a proper action: both that aspect of it by virtue of which it engages in modifications of the sort of which the proper action is an example, and that aspect of it by virtue of which it engages in modifications that cause modifications of the sort of which the proper action is an example. Proper actions are revelatory of more about a substance's nature than any passion could be, and it is because of this that proper actions are more strongly attributable to substances than passions.[9]

We now have an account of the way in which Locke's distinction between proper action and passion lends insight into the problem of agency: The distinction does not yet draw the line between doings and happenings, but it draws a line between two different degrees of attributability of modifications, and, by doing so, makes a first step toward understanding the kind of deep attributability, attributability to persons, that is characteristic of doings. What this suggests is that the kind of attributability we are after might be a special case of the broadly natural phenomenon of proper action. If so, then Locke's distinction between passion and proper action contains an important insight that it is easy to overlook when thinking about agency: Human beings (and other animals) are not the only creatures capable of instantiating agency-like characteristics. There is something like agency—although not full-fledged agency itself—occurring in seemingly inert parts of the natural world: the sun, for instance, expresses its active powers.

Further, Locke sees human agency as a special case of the widely occurring phenomenon of proper action: The subset of proper actions that are most strongly attributable to the beings in which they inhere—those that we think of as "deeds" or "doings"—are what Locke calls "voluntary actions." In Locke's account, naturally, a voluntary action is voluntary by virtue of the fact that it bears an intimate relationship to a volition. (It follows that the only beings capable of having modifications that are attributable in this deepest sense are those that are capable of having volitions.) But understanding what relationship holds between such modifications and volitions and why this makes these modifications attributable in some special way to the agents in which they inhere—more deeply attributable to such creatures than the proper actions of a windup toy are attributable to the toy—requires understanding Locke's account of volition. Therefore, it is to that account that I turn in the next section.

WHAT ARE VOLITIONS?

Volitions, for Locke, are acts of the mind. Things that lack minds do not ever have volitions. Acts of the mind are to be distinguished from ideas, the objects of the mind. Acts of the mind are modifications of substances that may or may not be proper actions. Locke makes this point in the following passage (quoted earlier):

> [A] Power to receive *Ideas* or Thoughts, from the operation of any external substance, is called a *Power* of thinking: but this is but a *Passive Power*, or Capacity. But to be able to bring into view *Ideas* out of sight at one's own choice, and to compare which of them one thinks fit, this is an *Active Power*. (II.XXI.72)

The mind has the power to receive ideas from external objects, and a particular reception of an idea from an object is an act of the mind. However, this act is not a proper action, for it is expressive only of a passive power of the mind. On the other hand, the mind has the power to turn its attention toward a particular idea in accordance with a choice to do so. A particular case of turning one's attention toward an idea as a result of a choice to do so is an act of the mind, and it is a proper action, since it is caused by another modification of the mind, namely, the choice or volition to do so.

Most volitions (in fact, probably all volitions that have ever actually occurred) are proper actions, for volitions are, Locke believes, caused by uneasinesses, and our uneasinesses are modifications of ourselves.[10] It follows, then, that volitions are expressive of an active power in us, a power to produce volitions, that is, the will.

But we have come little closer to understanding exactly what volitions are. Locke says some instructive things about the nature of volition. For instance:

> *Volition*, 'tis plain, is an Act of the Mind knowingly exerting that Dominion it takes itself to have over any part of the man, by imploying it in, or withholding it from, any particular Action. (II.XXI.15)

> *Volition* is nothing but that particular determination of the mind, whereby, barely by a thought the mind endeavours to give rise, continuation, or stop, to any Action which it takes to be in its power. (II.XXI.30)

One thing that emerges from these passages is that Locke seems to think that volition is *self-consciously* aimed at the production of action. If the mind "knowingly exert[s] that Dominion it takes itself to have over . . . the man" in volition, then it would seem that for an act of my mind to count as a volition, I need to be "taking" my mind to have control over some part of myself when I engage in the act. That is, I must believe that my mind is hooked up to my body (or some other part of myself) in such a way that my body will, generally, move when my mind issues the command to move. It is a necessary condition for a particular act of my mind to count as a volition that I conceive of it in a particular way: namely, as an exercise of my ability to control my body (or some other part of myself). Let's call this the Conception Condition on volition. (I express this condition with greater precision below.)[11]

So, an act of the mind does not count as a volition simply by virtue of its intrinsic, nonrelational properties. That is, we could demote a mental act from its status as a volition without changing the mental act itself, merely by changing the surrounding psychological facts. This is analogous to the way in which we might demote a particular vocal utterance from its status as an act of communication by changing the psychological facts of the speaker; the very same sound uttered in the very same way might be an act of communication if the speaker has certain beliefs about language and otherwise not. The existence of such beliefs are facts about the mental context of occurrence of the relevant utterance that contribute to the utterance qualifying as an act of communication. Analogously, the Conception Condition is a condition on the mental context of occurrence of the mental act that counts as a volition; the very same mental act could occur without satisfaction of the Conception Condition, and in such an instance, the mental act would not count as a volition. So, a mental act that precedes and causes a particular proper action need not be a volition at all, even if it would have been a volition had the appropriate contextual condition been satisfied. It follows that I can engage in a proper action caused by an act of my mind that is in all intrinsic respects identical to a volition without ever having had a volition to so act, if I failed to satisfy the Conception Condition.

What this implies is that Locke has a resource for understanding certain cases of quite peculiar action, such as sleepwalking: sleepwalking is purposive action—it isn't like a heartbeat or a reflex action—but it doesn't seem to be fully voluntary.[12] Under Locke's account of the nature of volition, sleepwalking is not normally caused by a volition at all, for while it may be caused by an act of the mind that is in all intrinsic respects identical to a volition, it is quite rare that the Conception Condition would be satisfied in such cases. Locke is then able to say exactly what we want to say: cases of sleepwalking are like voluntary actions in certain respects, and different in others. The sleepwalker's walking bears a relation to a volition-like state by virtue of which the walking is similar to a voluntary action, but as the volition-like state is not a full-fledged volition, the action is not a full-fledged voluntary action.

These remarks might be extended to understand the actions of some animals as well: it is an empirical issue whether or not (or which) animals can and do satisfy the Conception Condition, but it seems more or less clear that some animals do not. It follows that, say, a spider's web-spinning is related to a state of the spider that is something like a volition, but not a full-fledged volition, and hence the web-spinning cannot be a full-fledged voluntary action, despite the fact that it is closer to being a voluntary action than, say, an amoeba's response to light.

What we have so far is a claim about a particular relational property that an act of the mind must have for it to count as a volition: It must satisfy the Conception Condition, but Locke also has things to say about the intrinsic properties of volitions; that is, he has things to say not just about the context in which the mental act must occur to be a volition, but also about what the mental act itself must be like for it to count as a volition:

> *Volition* or *Willing* is an act of the Mind directing its thought to the production of any Action, and thereby exerting its power to produce it. (II.XXI.28)

This remark suggests two claims about the nature of volition. The first is that to have a volition is to turn one's attention toward the idea of the production of an action.[13] The second claim is that to have a volition is to exert a power to produce the action. The two claims together suggest that to have a volition is to turn one's attention toward the idea of the production of an action, and that act of turning one's attention is itself an exertion of a power to produce the action.

This leads quickly to an objection: Under this conception of volition, mustn't all volitions be successful in order to even count as volitions? The trouble is that if the act of turning one's attention toward the idea of the production of a particular action is itself the exertion of a power to produce that action, then the agent must have the power to produce the action and also be exerting that power. In which case, it would seem to follow that the action actually occurs, since if it failed to occur, then that would be decisive evidence that the agent did not in fact have the power to so act. We can understand how an agent could have a power to act in a particular way and not act that way *if she failed to exert her power to so act*, but how could an agent possibly have a power to act in a particular way, exert the power, and yet not so act? Locke is not likely to have made it a condition on the having of a volition that the volition be successful, however, for he is quite clear that an agent can have a volition (not just a putative volition, but a real volition) while lacking the power to act in accordance with the volition. For instance, he says:

> [A] Man falling into the Water, (a Bridge breaking under him), has not herein liberty, is not a free agent. For though he has Volition, though he prefers his not falling to falling; yet the forbearance of that Motion not being in his Power, the Stop or Cessation of that Motion follows not upon his Volition. (II.XXI.9)

And, even more explicitly:

> I readily recognize ineffective volition, as when a paralytick wills to move his palsied hand; I grant that that volition is ineffective and without result.[14]

Is Locke simply inconsistent, or is there a way to understand his account of the intrinsic nature of volition under which volitions need not be successful? I believe the latter. Let me elaborate.

A first question to ask about Locke's account of the intrinsic nature of volition is this: What are exertions of power? Since volitions are themselves, according to Locke, exertions of a power to produce an action, in order to understand what volitions are supposed to be, we need to understand what an exertion of a power is. Locke does not offer an account of the nature of exertions of power,[15] but it seems that we can offer an account for him that is consistent with his other views.[16] Say a substance S has an active power to A, where A is a type of modification of the substance itself or another substance. When a modification of type A actually occurs, it is caused not by the *power* to A, but by an *exertion* of that power—where the exertion is an (often observable) event. That is, let's call the modification of S that causes a modification of type A (in a case in which such a modification actually occurs) an exertion of S's power to A. The exertion itself is caused by other states or events, but it would not have been so caused had it not been for the power to A in S. That is, the power is the state of S by virtue of which the exertion is conceptually explicable; it is an enabling condition for the occurrence of the exertion; the power is that state of the substance by virtue of which it engaged (in the imagined situation) in a modification of the type of which the exertion is a token. If we call the type of modification of which the exertion is a token E, it is correct to say that the active power to A is also a passive power to E. Further, the passive power to E is rightly called an active power to A only if the relevant exertion does indeed bring about a modification of type A. What this means is that the same state of the agent by virtue of which the exertion is explicable—the passive power to E—can count as an active power to A on one occasion and not on another, despite the fact that it is itself no different on one occasion than on the other. For instance, imagine that I have a volition to raise my arm[17] and it causes my arm to rise. Call my passive power to have this volition P; P is that state of me by virtue of which the volition is explicable; P is that state of me (we-know-not-what) by virtue of which I have a volition to raise my arm. In the example under consideration, in which my arm does in fact rise, P is an active power to raise my arm. However, we can imagine an alternative circumstance in which I have a volition to raise my arm, but my arm fails to rise (perhaps I'm tied down). The volition might still be explicable by virtue of state P; that is, P would still be a passive power to have the relevant volition. P would then not rightly be called an active power to raise my arm. So, if I'm tied down and have a volition to raise my arm, I might be (somewhat imprecisely) said to be exerting my power to raise my arm while at the same time not raising my arm, for I am exerting a power that would count as a power to raise my arm in an appropriate circumstance of which the current circumstance is not an example.

So what does Locke mean when he says that the mental act of turning one's attention toward the idea of the production of a particular action must be an "exertion" of a power to produce the action in order for the mental act to count as a volition? Maybe what he means is that the mental act of turning one's attention must be explicable by virtue of a state of the agent that would, in some circumstance, count as an active power to produce an action of the relevant type. So, the relevant state of the agent needn't actually be, in the current circumstance, an active power to A; it need only be such that it would count as such a power in the appropriate circumstances: circumstances in which an exertion of the power did indeed cause a modification of type A.

We now have a response to the earlier objection. The objection was that on Locke's account of the intrinsic nature of volition—in which a mental act is not a volition unless the agent has a power of which the volition is an exertion—all volitions are successful. But, if we understand exertions of power in the manner that I am suggesting, then we have an account of the intrinsic nature of volition under which volitions needn't be successful: All that is required for the exertion to be an exertion of a power to A is that the relevant state of the agent, which makes the occurrence of the volition conceptually explicable (that is, the passive power to have such a volition), would count as a power to A in appropriate circumstances (of which the current circumstances may or may not be an example).

If we think of the intrinsic nature of volition in this way, then, how are we to understand the Conception Condition? That is, how must the agent conceive of the mental act that is the exertion of the power for that mental act to count as a volition? Locke repeatedly expresses the Conception Condition by saying that it is important that the action be one that the mind "takes to be in its power." The trouble is that this phrase is ambiguous between two interpretations: In the first, it means that the agent must believe, or be aware, that her passive power to have the volition is an active power to act *in this very circumstance*; in the second interpretation, it means only that the agent takes her passive power to have the volition to count, in *normal* circumstances (of which the current circumstances may or may not turn out to be an example), as an active power to act.

Locke was probably not clear, himself, on this issue. However, I think that the remarks regarding the Conception Condition push more toward the second of these two interpretations. Locke uses the phrase the "[d]ominion [the mind] takes itself to have over any part of the man" (II.XXI.15). This sounds like the mind takes itself to have, *in general*, a certain kind of control over certain parts of the person's mind or body. But this needn't involve belief, or some other kind of awareness, that the mind has such control *in this very circumstance*, but only that the relevant power is, in general, an active power to act. (It also may require that the agent *lacks* a belief that this very circumstance is *not* a normal circumstance.) I am not entirely certain that this is the correct interpretation, but it is the most natural interpretation. Further, there is a philosophical reason to accept the latter rather than the former account of the Conception Condition:

Michael Bratman has offered a number of rationality conditions on intention, conditions, that is, that must be satisfied if the agent's intentions are to be rational. (I am assuming here and later that intentions and volitions do not differ meaningfully.) One of these conditions is what Bratman calls the "strong consistency" condition: You cannot rationally intend to do A if you believe that you will not do A. This is not to be confused with the view upheld by some philosophers (Grice is one example[18]) that if you intend to do A, then you must believe that you will. Bratman's condition is weaker than this, for under it you could intend to do A, fail to believe that you will, and also fail to believe that you won't, without falling into irrationality.[19]

Bratman notes that for there to be meaningful rationality conditions on intention, it must be possible to have *irrational* intentions. That is, it must not be constitutive of a mental state's counting as an intention that it satisfy conditions such as the strong consistency condition. If Locke accepts the first of the two interpretations of the Conception Condition (the interpretation under which the agent must believe that her passive power to have the volition is, in this very circumstance, an active power to act), then an agent cannot be rightly said to have a volition at all when she fails to meet the strong consistency condition, for if she lacks the belief that she will act, she will not satisfy the Conception Condition. On the other hand, if Locke accepts the second interpretation of the Conception Condition (under which the agent need only believe that her passive power to have the volition is, in general, an active power to act), then it will be possible for the agent to have an irrational volition, for the agent might have the relevant general belief and also believe that, in this circumstance, the relevant power is not an active power to act. This provides, then, a philosophical reason for Locke to hold the Conception Condition under its second interpretation. Obviously, I don't think that this is evidence for thinking that Locke had a clear view one way or the other. My point is only that the second interpretation is more philosophically appealing than the first, and the texts are more naturally interpreted in accordance with it.[20]

Here, then, is a textually consistent, and philosophically appealing, interpretation of Locke's account of volition. In this definition, S is an agent, V is an act of S's mind, P is S's passive power to engage in acts of the type of which V is a token, and A is a type of modification:

> V is a volition to A *if and only if* (1) V is the turning of S's attention toward an idea of the production of A, (2) if V were to occur in a normal circumstance in which it caused a modification of type A, P would count as an active power to A, and (3) (Conception Condition) S believes, or is in some other way aware, that, in general (that is, in most circumstances), P is an active power to A, and that V is an exertion of P.[21]

The motivating idea of this account of volition is this: When we have a volition, all we do is turn our attention toward the idea of the production of the action. But in order for that act to count as a volition, it needs to bear the appropriate relation to an important state of ourselves—a state that would count as an active power in the right circumstances and counts as (at least) a passive power in these—and we must take that state to be, usually, an active power to act as our volition directs.[22]

It is of importance to note that this account of volition, spe-
cifically the addition of the Conception Condition, marked a
change in Locke's view. In the first edition of the *Essay*, Locke
offered a much less sophisticated account of volition than the
account that I have just described. (The account just described
appears in the second and later editions of the *Essay*.) For instance, the passage from the second and later editions quoted
earlier (the passage from II.XXI.15) changed drastically from
its first edition incarnation. Here is how it reads in the second
and later editions:

> *Volition*, 'tis plain, is an Act of the Mind knowingly exerting that
> Dominion it takes itself to have over any part of the man, by im-
> ploying it in, or withholding it from, any particular Action.
> (II.XXI.15)

And here is how it reads in the first edition:

> *Volition*, 'tis plain, is nothing but the actual choosing or preferring
> the forbearance to the doing, or doing to the forbearance, of any
> particular Action in our power, that we think on. (II.XXI.15, first
> edition.)

The Conception Condition was not mentioned in the first edition. (The other passage quoted above in which the Conception
Condition is mentioned—the passage from II.XXI.30—is simply absent in the first edition.)

Locke also had a much less sophisticated view of the intrinsic
nature of volition in the first edition. Again, the passage that I
quoted earlier from the second and later editions changed radically from the first edition. Here is the passage as it appears in
the second and later editions:

> *Volition* or *Willing* is an act of the Mind directing its thought to
> the production of any Action, and thereby exerting its power to
> produce it. (II.XXI.28)

In the first edition, the entire section was different, so more
than just this passage was replaced, but here is what Locke said
about volition in the first edition section:

> *Volition* or *Willing*, regarding only what is in our power, *is* nothing but the *preferring* the doing of any thing, to the not doing of it; Action to Rest, *et contra*. Well, but what is this *Preferring*? It *is* nothing but the *being pleased more with the one, than the other.* (II.XXI.28, first edition)

The view of volition that Locke was working with in the first edition is far less sophisticated than the view that he offered in the second and later editions. The first edition view seems to be little more than this: Anytime we prefer one action to another (both of which are in our power), we are having a volition in favor of that action. This account of volition captures a much wider class of mental acts than the later, more sophisticated account captures. For instance, there are times when I prefer to do something but make no effort at all to do it, nor do I think that the preferring of it might be causally efficacious in bringing the act about. Such desiderative states would count as volitions according to the first edition account of volition, while they would fail to count as volitions (for a variety of reasons) under the account of the second and later editions.[23]

A Quick Look Back

What have I done so far in this chapter? I have argued that Locke's distinction between passion and proper action is a first step toward a solution to the problem of agency as it identifies a distinction in degrees of attributability of modifications to substances of which full-fledged agency will be a particular instance. And—in order to prepare the way for understanding Locke's account of the nature of full-fledged agency, his account of voluntary action—I have given an interpretation of Locke's account of volition under which a volition involves, among other things, a self-conscious awareness on the part of the agent of the causal role of the volition in the production of action. The next task is to show what role Locke's account of volition plays in his account of voluntary action.

VOLUNTARY ACTION

Voluntariness is a property of some of the states and events in which we engage; the states and events that possess this property do so by virtue of the relationship they bear to some volition. But what relationship must hold between a volition and a particular modification of an agent if that modification is to count as a voluntary action? There are very few places in Locke's texts that are relevant for assessing his view on this matter. The text that offers the closest thing to a definition of voluntary action is as follows:

> The forbearance or performance of [any] action, consequent to such order or command of the mind [that is, a volition], is called *Voluntary*. And whatsoever action is performed without such a thought of the mind, is called *Involuntary*. (II.XXI.5)

A first question to ask is what role, for Locke, causation by volition plays in making a modification of an agent into a voluntary action. E. J. Lowe has offered the following interpretation of Locke's view of voluntary action:[24]

> A modification A of an agent S is voluntary *if and only if* it is caused by a volition to A on the part of S.

Under this interpretation, Locke is making two claims: a claim that causation by volition is necessary for an action to be voluntary, and a claim that it is sufficient. As I argue below, Lowe is right in attributing the first of these claims to Locke, but wrong in attributing the second. More is needed, in Locke's account, for the voluntariness of an action than mere causation by volition.[25] But what more is needed? There is very little in Locke's texts to go on, but, as I will argue, if we take seriously the account of volition that I have attributed to Locke, it is a short step to an account of the relationship that must hold between a volition and a modification for the modification to be a voluntary action.

The Necessity of Causation by Volition
for Voluntariness

Here is an objection to the proposition, which both Lowe and I hold, that for Locke all voluntary actions are caused by volitions to do them:

Locke says, "[T]he sitting still, even of a Paralytic, whilst he prefers it to a removal, is truly voluntary." (II.XXI.11) A natural way to think of a person who has been paralyzed is to think of the mechanism that allows her volitions to cause movements in her body to have been damaged or destroyed. If we think of paralysis in this way, then the paralyzed person's volitions do not cause her physical states at all, even when they are volitions to sit still; they can't have any causal influence on her sitting still, for they have such causal influence only by virtue of a mechanism that is not operative. Under this account of paralysis, the result of being paralyzed is this: Both movement and absence of movement are taken out of the agent's control—neither follow from volitions on the part of the agent—for whatever links between the mind and the body that were necessary for the production of such modifications have been damaged. However, Locke is quite clear that if a paralyzed person has a volition to sit still and sits still, then her action is voluntary. But if Locke is thinking of paralysis in the way just described, then he cannot have thought that a volition must cause an action in order for the action to count as voluntary, for the paralyzed person's volitions cannot exert any causal influence on (a certain range of)[26] her actions.

Since Locke's remark about paralysis appears in the first edition, it is possible that it is merely a slip left over from his first edition account of volition. Recall that in the first edition, Locke took volitions to be no more than preferences: anytime an agent has a positive attitude toward a course of conduct, she is having a volition in favor of that course of conduct. Under this account of volition, volitions aren't exertions, they aren't efforts to produce conduct, and thus it is natural to suggest that a modification would count as a voluntary action whenever the agent does indeed favor the modification, even if the modification is not caused by the preference.[27] Thus, a paralyzed person's sitting still would be voluntary despite the fact that it is not a causal consequence of her preference in favor of it, since voluntariness never requires, on this view, causation by volition. Thus, we might respond to the objection by dismissing Locke's remark about paralysis on the grounds that it expresses an account of voluntary action that fits naturally with his first edition account of volition rather than with the account that he came, eventually, to favor. While this is one possible way to respond to the objection, I hesitate to endorse it, largely because Locke altered his remarks about volition in the second edition with such care and precision that it seems unlikely he would have overlooked this needed excision.

There is another response to the objection available—a response under which Locke's remark about paralysis remains consistent with his second edition account of volition—for there is another way we might think about paralysis under which the paralyzed person's volition to sit still might indeed be one of the causes of her sitting still. All of us have physical limitations; I cannot jump high enough to dunk a basketball, for instance. But it would be bizarre to conclude from the fact that I cannot jump a certain height that my volitions are not causally efficacious in the production of any actions that are incompatible with jumping such a height. After all, if I choose to jump up two feet rather than the four necessary for dunking the basketball, then I will jump up two feet; jumping roughly two feet high is incompatible with jumping roughly four feet high. So, there are actions incompatible with jumping four feet high that might come about as a result of my choosing to so act. Now, it is agreed on all sides that a person who is paralyzed cannot move, but does that show that the paralyzed person's volitions cannot be causally efficacious in the production of actions incompatible with moving? No, for we could not make the analogous inference from my inability to jump a certain height to an inability on my part to perform any action incompatible with so jumping; it follows that there is no reason to think that we can make the inference in the case of the paralyzed person. So, a volition to sit still (sitting still is an action incompatible with moving) on the part of the paralyzed person might play a causal role in her sitting still.

To put the point slightly differently: In me there is some route connecting a volition to jump with certain jumping movements (perhaps this is a neural path, perhaps a path from my immaterial mind through my pituitary gland to my body, who knows?). Let's say that that route is "in place" if there are *some* jumping movements that will come about if I choose to jump. To say that the route is in place is not to say that *any* jumping movement that I choose will in fact come about—a choice to jump four feet, for instance, would not be effective. Now let's think about the paralyzed person. If the route from volitions to move to movement is not in place in the paralyzed person, then Locke cannot both hold that the paralyzed person who chooses to sit still does so voluntarily, *and* that causation of action by volition is necessary for voluntariness, since, after all, sitting still is a form of movement (just as a single point is an example of a line). But, there is an alternative way of thinking about paralysis: The route from volitions to move to movements is in place in the paralyzed person but it has limited functionality; it is only useful for producing one form of movement: sitting still. So, Locke could quite consistently hold both that causation of an action by volition is necessary for voluntariness and hold that the paralyzed person who chooses to sit still does so voluntarily, just so long as he also holds a particular conception of paralysis, a conception under which the relevant route is in place in the paralyzed person but has limited functionality (just as the route from volitions to jump to jumping movements is in place in me, but has limited functionality).

Locke is committed to this—somewhat forced[28]—conception of paralysis if he holds that causation by volition is necessary for voluntariness, and if his remark about the paralyzed person is not a slip. One thing to note is that under this conception of paralysis, the example of the paralyzed person who chooses to sit still is structurally identical to the case of the man in the locked room who decides to stay. In the man in the locked room case, there are two circumstances either of which would be enough by itself to cause his staying: his volition to stay and the lock on the door. In the case of the paralyzed man, there are also two circumstances either of which would be enough by itself to cause his action: his volition to sit still and his inability to do anything else. The assimilation of these two cases is evidence in favor of attributing the second conception of paralysis to Locke, for Locke thinks that both examples indicate the same thing: that it is possible to act voluntarily while being under necessity.

So we have a possible response to an objection to the claim that, for Locke, causation of action by volition is necessary for voluntariness, a response that maintains interpretive charity by avoiding the dismissal of Locke's remark about paralysis. But, in addition, there are a number of positive pieces of evidence in favor of the claim. The first is that Locke quite clearly thinks that voluntary actions are proper actions, and he thinks that voluntary actions are voluntary by virtue of their relationship (causal or not) to a volition to do them. Locke also thinks—as I've argued earlier—that proper actions are proper by virtue of the fact that their causes are internal to that in which the proper action inheres. But if he did not hold causation of action by volition to be necessary for voluntariness, then he would have to be asserting that voluntary actions are proper by virtue of some other modification of the agent (besides the agent's volition to do what she did) that caused them. Since Locke nowhere offers another candidate for the cause of voluntary actions by virtue of which they are proper actions, it seems quite strange to think that volitions aren't (or aren't necessarily) the causes of voluntary actions by virtue of which they are proper.

Another piece of evidence that favors the necessity of causation by volition to voluntariness is pointed out by Lowe. Lowe notes the following passage:

> All our voluntary Motions . . . are produced in us only by the free Action and Thought of our own Minds. . . . For example: My right Hand writes, whilst my left Hand is still: What causes rest in one, and motion in the other? Nothing but my Will, a Thought

of my Mind; my Thought only changing, the right Hand rests,
and the left Hand moves. (IV.X.19, also quoted in Lowe 1986,
150–51)

Notice that there is no implication in this passage of the *sufficiency* of causation by volition for voluntariness.[29] The claim is
that all voluntary motions possess a certain characteristic: they
are caused by volitions. But Locke does not commit himself to
the claim that all motions caused by volitions are voluntary.
Lowe, as I've said already, believes that, for Locke, causation of
action by volition is sufficient for voluntariness. I argue against
this claim in the next section.

The (Non)Sufficiency of Causation by
Volition for Voluntariness

The account of voluntary action that Lowe attributes to Locke
is not philosophically sound, because causation by volition simply isn't sufficient for voluntariness. The account runs into difficulties, in particular, from cases involving deviant causal
chains: If I have a volition to let go, and reflection on the fact
that I had such a volition causes me to become so nervous that
I let go, then my volition caused my letting go, despite the fact
that I did not do so voluntarily.[30] This does not show that Locke
did not hold the view that Lowe attributes to him—and it would
not be surprising if he had overlooked cases of this sort, for he
certainly failed to anticipate the notion of a deviant causal
chain. But, in fact, I don't think that Locke does hold that causation by volition is sufficient for the voluntariness of an action.
     My objection comes from Locke's remark regarding invol-
untary action: "[W]hatsoever action is performed without [a
volition], is called *Involuntary*." (II.XXI.5) What is Locke claiming in this passage?
     Under what I will call the First Interpretation of the passage,
Locke is claiming *only* that if an action is performed and no
volition to perform the action precedes it, then the action is
involuntary. Under this First Interpretation, Locke is claiming
that absence of an appropriate volition is sufficient for the in-

voluntariness of an action. This is the contrapositive of the claim that causation by volition is necessary for voluntary action (assuming that involuntary is the same as not-voluntary—more on this shortly), a claim Locke seems to have made. So, under the First Interpretation, the remark counts as positive evidence only for the claim that causation by volition is necessary for voluntary action, and we still have no evidence one way or the other as to what Locke took to be sufficient conditions for voluntariness. The trouble with this interpretation is that it means that Locke never (as far as I know) explicitly offered necessity conditions for *involuntary* action (that is, sufficiency conditions for *voluntary* action). Perhaps this is right, but it is rather disappointing, for it means that Locke left an important lacuna in his philosophy of action, despite his explicit reliance (in, for instance, II.XXVIII.4, II.XXVIII.5, II.XXVIII.14) on the concept of voluntary action. In addition, the remark concerning involuntary action seems to be taken by Locke to be a definition rather than just a reiteration of a claim made in the preceding sentence (namely, that causation by volition is necessary for voluntariness). A textually consistent interpretation that sees Locke as having offered some set of sufficiency conditions on voluntary action is to be preferred to the First Interpretation.

Here is a Second Interpretation of the remark:

> *Second Interpretation*: A modification of an agent is an involuntary action *if and only if* the agent had no volition in favor of the modification.

If the Second Interpretation captures Locke's meaning, then he cannot have consistently held the view that Lowe attributes to him. He cannot, that is, have held that causation by volition is sufficient for voluntariness. The problem is as follows:

As I've argued already, Locke does hold that causation by volition is necessary for voluntariness; that is, he does hold that the following conditional is true: If an action is voluntary, then it was caused by a volition to do it. This suggests two sufficient ways for an action to be not-voluntary: the action could be preceded by a volition that failed to cause it,[31] or the action could be preceded by no volition at all. Under the Second Interpretation, actions that are preceded by volitions that are not causally responsible for them are not-involuntary, and that seems to suggest that such actions would be voluntary. So, Locke seems to be holding an inconsistent position: He seems to be holding (as a consequence of his view that causation by volition is necessary for voluntary action) that actions preceded by volitions that did not cause them are involuntary, while at the same time holding (as a consequence of his putative view that involuntary actions are not even preceded by volitions to do them) that such actions are voluntary. So, if Locke held the view of involuntary action described in the Second Interpretation, his position is inconsistent.

It is possible that Locke just overlooked the possibility of cases in which an agent has a volition to do something, does it, and yet the volition failed to cause the action. But such cases are not so peculiar, so it is not quite clear why he would have overlooked them, especially since he was aware of causal overdetermination cases (the man in the locked room and the paralyzed person are examples) that are similar in a variety of respects.

One way to defend the Second Interpretation is to suggest that Locke thinks that there are three categories delineated in his account of voluntary action: the voluntary, the involuntary, and the nonvoluntary.[32] If Locke did hold that there are three categories defined by his account of voluntary action, then actions preceded but not caused by volitions would count as nonvoluntary, and it would be correct to say (as the Second Interpretation does) that the involuntary are all those actions that are not preceded by volitions to do them. There are two problems with this move. First, as far as I can tell, there is no textual evidence for thinking that this is what Locke had in mind. The definition of voluntary action that he offers reads as though it were meant to be a binary criterion: all actions are either voluntary or involuntary. Further, this appearance is strengthened by the title that Locke gives to section 11: "*Voluntary opposed to involuntary, not to Necessary.*" (II.XXI.11) If Locke thought that there were three categories, then voluntary would not be "opposed" only to involuntary but also to nonvoluntary. There is a second problem as well: The tripartite distinction between the voluntary, involuntary, and nonvoluntary is usually drawn in order to aid in the classification of, for instance, the modifications of inert objects. Such modifications are certainly not voluntary actions, but, we might think, nor are they involuntary actions; they are modifications to which the distinction between the voluntary and the involuntary does not apply. However, if this is the purpose that the tripartite distinction is meant to serve, what could possibly justify the claim that modifications that are preceded by volitions that do not cause them are nonvoluntary? After all, the nonvoluntary was supposed to apply to the modifications of things incapable of having volitions at all. It is possible, I suppose, that the tripartite distinction was being relied on by Locke for some other purpose that remains undisclosed, but it seems a rather absurd stretch to attribute Locke with reliance on a tripartite distinction that is both textually and philosophically unsupported.[33]

Lowe would probably want to avoid the inconsistency between the Second Interpretation and his claim that, for Locke, causation by volition is sufficient for voluntariness by returning to the First Interpretation: the interpretation under which the remark about involuntary action is a statement only of the necessity of causation by volition for voluntary action. As I've argued above, I don't think that that is the best interpretation of the remark. It is, however, a better interpretation than the Second Interpretation under which Locke is straightforwardly inconsistent. But, in fact, I think there is a third interpretation that is better still. Further, what emerges is an account of Locke's view of voluntary action that differs from Lowe's, and under which Locke has a resource for responding to the deviant causal chain cases that plague the account that Lowe attributes to him. Or, at least, so I argue in the next section.

An Alternative Interpretation

The remark regarding involuntary action was absent from the first edition of the *Essay*.[34] Further, as I've argued above, the first edition of the *Essay* offered a rather different, and far less sophisticated account of volition than Locke offered in the second and later editions. I believe that the second edition account of volition can be used to understand Locke's remark about involuntary action.

First, let's distinguish between a volition causing an action, and an action satisfying the content of a volition. Volitions, under almost any account of their nature, have propositional content; they describe a particular state of affairs as to-be-achieved. Let's say that a volition is "satisfied" just in case the state of affairs that it describes does, in fact, come about. Under the account of volition that Locke offered in the first edition of the *Essay*—the account in which a volition is nothing but a preference in favor of a particular action—my head nodding would satisfy my volition to nod my head, even if the volition played no role in causing my head to nod. The reason for this is that if my volition is merely a preference favoring a particular modification of myself (the nodding of my head), then that preference is fulfilled regardless of how it comes about that I nod my head. The preference could be fulfilled, in fact, even if you grasp my head and nod it for me, as it were. The satisfaction condition for a volition, under the first edition account of volition, is merely the occurrence of that act which the volition favors.[35] But what are the satisfaction conditions for a volition under the second edition account of volition, as I have reconstructed it? Or, to put the question a different way, what state of affairs does a volition describe as to-be-achieved under the account of volition offered in the second edition?

Here is a suggestion—as before, S is an agent, V is a volition to A, P is S's passive power to engage in acts of the type of which V is a token, and A is a type of modification:

> V is satisfied *if and only if* (1) S A's, and (2) it follows from the fact that A occurred in the manner that it occurred that P is an active power to A and that V is an exertion of that power (i.e., the agent's conception of her volition is confirmed by the occurrence of A).

For the second of these two conditions to be fulfilled, the agent's A-ing must have come about as a result of the agent turning her attention toward the production of her action, that is, as a result of her volition. Further, the agent's conception of her volition as the exertion of a power that is, usually, an active power to A must be confirmed by the occurrence of the action.[36] The action's occurrence will not confirm the agent's conception of her volition unless the volition causes her action in a particular way, in the way that the agent expects her volition to cause her action, the way through which her action would indicate that P is an active power to A. If the agent's volition is satisfied, then the volition did in fact cause the action. Causing an action, however, is not necessarily enough for the satisfaction of a volition, for the volition could cause an action in a way quite different from the way the agent conceived of the action as being caused, a way that failed to indicate that P is an active power to A.

I suggest that this is Locke's conception of voluntary action:

> A proper action A of an agent S is voluntary *if and only if* it satisfies a volition to A on the part of S.

One piece of rather weak textual evidence for this interpretation comes from Locke's definition of voluntary action. In that definition, he says that the voluntary actions are those that are performed "consequent to" (II.XXI.5) a volition. This is a peculiar phrase and suggests that he wanted to avoid using the language of causation when offering his sufficiency condition for voluntary action. The remark is, of course, inconclusive, but I think that it suggests that things are more complicated than Lowe allows. Further, Locke repeatedly refers to "accord" between one's volition and one's action when that action is voluntary (cf. II.XXI.8, II.XXI.10, II.XXI.12, II.XXI.13, II.XXI.15, II.XXI.27, II.XXI.71). This, also, is a rather peculiar turn of phrase, although it suggests something like the notion of satisfaction that I am invoking. Be that as it may, there are other reasons to accept my interpretation.

Notice that if Locke held the view of voluntary action that I am attributing to him, then his account of voluntary action is not falsified by cases involving deviant causal chains. Imagine, as before, that I have a volition to let go and reflection on the fact that I had such a volition causes me to become so nervous that I let go. Under the account that Lowe attributes to Locke, such an action will count, incorrectly, as a voluntary action. However, on the account that I am attributing to Locke, it would not, for the action of letting go does not satisfy my volition. In particular, it does not follow from the manner of occurrence of the action that the relevant power of myself (the power by virtue of which I had the volition to let go) is an active power, for the letting go was not caused by the volition in the appropriate way, the way through which the relevant power would be expressed as an active power.

Let me put this point a different way: For my letting go to have been a voluntary action, that aspect of myself that accounts for the fact that I engage in volitions to let go must also account for the fact that I did, in fact, let go. But, if my letting go is accounted for in part by appeal to the fact that I got nervous, then the aspect of myself that explains why I got nervous—my passive power to get nervous—is also involved in accounting for the occurrence of my letting go. The result is that there is no saying, on the basis of the fact that I willed to let go and did so, whether or not the aspect of myself that accounts for my volition to let go is, in fact, an active power to let go. It follows that my letting go was not a voluntary action.

Another point in favor of the account of voluntary action that I am attributing to Locke is that it helps to account for the evidence to the effect that Locke thought that it is a necessary condition of an action's being voluntary that it was caused by a volition to do it, for it is a necessary condition of a volition's satisfaction that it causes the action that it is aimed at.

And, as I've already hinted, I believe that my interpretation helps to explain Locke's remark about involuntary action, which could not be explained adequately under Lowe's interpretation. The remark, recall, is this: "[W]hatsoever action is performed without such a thought of the mind [a volition to do it], is called *Involuntary*." (II.XXI.5) I suggest that the remark be interpreted as follows:

An action that satisfies a volition to do it also expresses the volition, indicates the presence in the agent of the prior volition. Such actions could be called actions that are performed *with volition*. Here, "with volition" means that the volition can be seen in the action itself; the action bears such a close relationship to the volition to do it (the relationship is captured by the satisfaction relation) that we can think of the action as almost containing the volition, as having been performed *with* the volition. Conversely, actions that do not bear the intimate relation of satisfaction to some previous volition can be thought of as actions performed "without volition." We might put it this way: Some actions indicate the presence of volition-in-action; they are performed with volitions; others do not; they are performed without volitions. So, Locke's remark about involuntary action ends up being a statement of the view that I am attributing to him: Locke is saying that involuntary actions are those that do not express volition; they are actions "without volition." Under my interpretation, the remark about involuntary action becomes a trivial consequence of the account of voluntary action, for if voluntary actions are all and only those actions that satisfy volitions to do them, then involuntary actions are surely all and only those that fail to so satisfy some relevant volition.

While it is true, I believe, that Locke held that voluntary actions are all and only those that satisfy volitions to do them, in the sense of "satisfy" that I have described, it is also true that he avoided putting this view in the forefront. There is a surreptitious quality to the remarks about voluntary and involuntary action: there are few of them, and Locke, uncharacteristically, avoids elaborating on the details and the implications of the account. I suspect that either Locke wanted to avoid argument over the issue, or else he was not himself fully aware that he held the view. Nonetheless, it is an account of voluntary action that is in the texts, and is philosophically more tenable than Lowe's natural alternative. What remains is to explain why it is that, under Locke's account, voluntary actions should be deeply attributable to agents in the way that we take them to be. It is to this issue that I will turn shortly, but first a short digression.

The Power to Act Voluntarily

Recall that one of the purposes of this chapter was to determine what criteria an agent must meet if she is to be rightly said to have the power to perform a particular action voluntarily. This power has particular importance for Locke, since it is one of the two powers that an agent must have if she is to have freedom of action with respect to a particular action. We are now in a position to offer such criteria.

Recall that it was both necessary and sufficient for the possession of a power that some particular conditional should be true of the agent. So, what conditional needs to be true of an agent if she is to have the power to act voluntarily? In the case of an active power to A, it is both necessary and sufficient for possession of the power at a particular time that if the agent were to exert the power, she would A; the exertion of the power has to be enough, in the circumstances, to bring about A. Voluntary actions are brought about by volitions, so at the very least, it is true of an agent who possesses an active power to voluntarily A that if she were to choose to A, she would A. However, that is not all that must be true of her, for mere causation by volition—as I've argued at length—is not sufficient for voluntary action. An A-ing must also fulfill the additional conditions specified in the satisfaction relation if it is to be voluntary. In short,

> An agent possesses an active power to voluntarily A *if and only if,* if she wills to A, she will A, and her A-ing will satisfy her volition to A.

The Special Attributability of Voluntary Action

Passions are all weakly attributable to the substances in which they inhere: they are expressive of the substance's passive power—something about the substance by virtue of which the modification occurred. Proper actions are more strongly attributable: they are expressive of the substance's active power—something about the substance by virtue of which both the modification and its causal source occurred. Voluntary actions are a species of proper actions, but they are attributable to their performers in some further elusive way that distinguishes them from the rest of the proper actions. But what is this further, special sort of attributability? And what is it about voluntary actions that makes them attributable to agents in this special way? The answers to these questions, I believe, lie in the Conception Condition and its connection to Locke's views on personal identity. Let me elaborate.

In addition to containing the changes in Locke's account of volition, the second edition of the *Essay* contains the chapter on personal identity (II.XXVII), absent from the first edition. The chapter on personal identity is aimed at providing an account of one of the conditions under which an action is appropriately attributable to a person, attributable in the way that supports judgments of responsibility.[37] Locke is insistent that such attribution is not the same as the attribution of properties to substances. This is one of the upshots of Locke's fervent argument against the view that personal identity consists in sameness of substance. Further, Locke insists that the special sort of attribution that supports judgments of responsibility is only justified where there is either awareness (of a sort discussed in chapter 3) of the relevant action or the possibility of producing such awareness in the agent to whom the action is being attributed. It is striking that in the second (and later) editions of the *Essay*, Locke presents a picture of volition under which volition is in part constituted by an act of reflective self-consciousness, and also presents a picture of personal identity in which the boundaries of the person are constituted by an act of reflective self-consciousness. Given Locke's interest in attributability in the personal identity chapter, it seems likely that the source of the deep attributability of voluntary actions lies in the fact that volitions, like the very boundaries of the person, are, in part, constituted by an act of reflective self-consciousness.

If choices, volitions, belong to us as persons—that is, are attributable to us in the elusive way in which past actions can be attributed to persons and never to mere animals—then those actions that are caused by and in accordance with choices may inherit this kind of belonging. If Locke is appealing to the same kind of self-consciousness in his account of personal identity and in his account of volition, then he has offered a tool for understanding the sense in which the actions of agents are distinctively self-revelatory and self-expressive: They are so by virtue of the fact that they are expressive of elements of our psyches that lie essentially within the boundaries of the person. Recall the difference between attribution of a proper action and attribution of a passion; the difference is a difference in degree: more about a creature is expressed by its proper actions than is expressed by its passions. The difference, for Locke, between attribution of a voluntary action and attribution of any other proper action is not a difference in degree, but a difference in kind: the former, and not the latter, is grounded in the teleological facts. I explain.

One of the great interpretive challenges of the personal identity chapter is to determine what kind of consciousness of action Locke is appealing to as being constitutive of personal identity. Many kinds of bare awareness of the occurrence of action are not going to be sufficient: if I am aware of the occurrence of your action, it doesn't become mine, or if I have a false memory, the imagined action does not then become something that I did. These kinds of awareness can't be the kind of awareness or self-consciousness that Locke takes to be constitutive of personal identity. But what kind of self-consciousness, then, does he have in mind?

In chapter 3, I try to make some headway on understanding what kind of awareness Locke takes to be constitutive of personal identity, but for now we need only say this much: The kind of awareness of one's volition and its role in the production of action that is specified explicitly in the Conception Condition doesn't ensure the kind of attributability that we are after. I could satisfy the Conception Condition (or a variant of it) with respect to a muscle spasm, but that would not mean that the arm movement caused by the spasm was attributable to me in any stronger way than any other proper action. What Locke's account of voluntary action requires, if it is really to account for the kind of deep attributability that we are trying to understand, is a richer account of the kind of self-consciousness that is involved both in constituting the boundaries of the person, and in constituting volition. Locke was probably right that *some* sort of self-consciousness is constitutive of the kind of strong attributability that we are trying to understand; the question is what kind of self-conscious awareness it is.

But, even without really understanding what kind of awareness Locke takes to be constitutive of personal identity, the mere fact that he appeals to such awareness as constitutive of volition helps us to understand what the special sense is in which our voluntary actions are attributable to us. Substances have a kind of unity across time; different properties of a substance held at different times are unified, are parts of a single thing, by virtue of some underlying thing, some substratum, that is the bearer of the properties at different times. Persons also have unity, but the unity is not metaphysical, but, if Locke is right, teleological.

Locke, famously, says:

> [Person] is a Forensick Term appropriating Actions and their Merit; and so belongs only to intelligent Agents capable of a Law, and Happiness and Misery. (II.XXVII.26)

The notion that the concept of a person is a concept of law seems, at first glance, rather peculiar. It might seem that even if there were no laws, either of our construction or God's, there could still be persons. But I believe Locke's point is this: The criterion for personal identity picks out as unified, as parts of a single being, a whole group of actions that occurred at various times. It picks out those actions that the agent can now become "conscious" of *only because* natural law demands that punishment and reward only be issued in such a way that the recipient is compelled to attribute to her present self *both* the past action and the punishment or reward (cf. II.XXVII.22, II.XXVII.26). It follows that if natural law made a different demand—if, for instance, justice demanded punishment of the very same *substance* that committed the crime—then personal identity would consist in something else: in, perhaps, the sameness of substance. Person is a "Forensick" concept in the deepest of senses: the very boundaries of the person depend on the content of natural law.

To say, then, that a past event is part of me as a person is to say that there is a law to which I am subject under which both the past event and the present events in which I am engaged are connected, are unified; in the clearest case, the unification relation is the "fitness" relation between punishment and crime. To make a choice, in Locke's account, is to be aware of one's action in the special way by virtue of which one is a subject of the laws and, thereby, to make the action arising out of the choice—the voluntary action—connected to oneself in the special way distinctive of agency. The attribution of voluntary action is quite different from the attribution of other proper actions: the former, and not the latter, is justified, when it is justified, only by virtue of the content of natural law.

Do the important parts of this picture survive rejection of Locke's natural law theory? The picture requires that there be important and indelible relations between crimes and later punishments that make those punishments appropriate to those crimes. That is, the unity of a person arises from the *appropriateness* of punishment of a particular substance awaiting judgment given a past action performed by a (possibly) different substance entirely. The punishment and the crime are unified—are parts of a single thing—only by virtue of the content of the "fitness" relation between punishment and crime; this relation, specified by natural law, is what makes it the case that both the crime and the later punishment belong to the same person. Thus, the special kind of attributability that voluntary actions enjoy is accounted for, in part, by appeal to a wholehearted belief in the coherence and truth of a retributivist conception of punishment, a conception that is an integral part of Locke's natural law theory. However, one could hold a retributivist conception of punishment without holding a natural law theory, and thus Locke's view regarding the special attribution of voluntary action does not depend on his natural law theory, but only upon the retributivism that it implies.[38]

Conclusion

What, then, was Locke's contribution to the problem of agency? Locke saw actions, in the contemporary sense of genuine doings, as being a special case of a more general phenomenon: external expressions of active powers. What this means, as I emphasized earlier, is that for Locke, agency in the fullest sense is continuous with related agency-like phenomena in the natural world. The kind of agency that we possess is not something irretrievably distant from that possessed by natural, unthinking objects. The kind of deep attributability typical of human actions is related by a stepwise progression to the kind of attributability to substances ubiquitous in the natural world. While this insight is not original with Locke—it is probably as old as the distinction between passion and action—it is a distinctive and evocative aspect of his conception of agency.

However, there is a way in which our agency is very different from that of nonpersons: Our actions, unlike those of beings incapable of thought, are brought about by certain crucial psychological elements. Further, what makes those psychological elements—that is, volitions—crucial is something constitutive of personhood: They are constituted in part by the occurrence of an act of self-conscious self-awareness of their role in the production of action. This, then, is Locke's primary contribution to the problem of agency: We are actors, *true* actors, not just because certain important elements of our psyches cause our behaviors, but also because we attribute those elements to ourselves—and thereby make them, and the actions arising out of them, the appropriate objects of natural laws—through a self-conscious awareness of their role in action.

3

Free Agency and Personal Identity

IN CHAPTER I, I argued that, for Locke, a full-fledged free agent is endowed with two sets of capacities: the capacity to adjust her conduct in accordance with her choices—freedom of action—and the capacity to adjust her choices in accordance with the good—freedom of will, improperly so called. We might put this conception of free agency this way: An agent is a full-fledged free agent when the world is dependent upon her in the right way, *and* she is dependent upon the world in the right way. For the world to be dependent on an agent in the right way, what she does must depend on what she chooses; for an agent to depend on the world in the right way, what she chooses must depend on what's good. Locke justifies the second claim—his account of the way in which the full-fledged free agent is dependent on the world—evaluatively; it is because determination of choice by the good is a *perfection* in the determination of choice that such determination is part of full-fledged free agency. Intuitively, the thought can be put like this: An agent whose volitions are determined by the good, or who at least possesses the ability to arrange such determination, can escape her own parochialisms and biases. She gives her will up—or is capable of giving her will up—to something better than herself, namely, the good, and thereby approaches divinity in her agency. I will argue here that the kinds of capacities that Locke takes to be constitutive of personal identity are closely related to both aspects of full-fledged free agency. What emerges is the following striking point: For Locke, it is through the right use of the capacities that make us persons that we become full-fledged free agents.

CHOICE AND PERSONAL IDENTITY

Part of our concern with free agency comes from a concern with autonomy. We want to be the source of our own actions; we want our actions to depend not on contingent features of our psychology or our circumstances, but on ourselves. In Locke's view, such dependency needn't be complete for full-fledged free agency; our choices can come about in part through forces external to ourselves, and we can still be full-fledged free agents. In fact, the possibility of giving oneself over to forces external to and better than oneself is a crucial aspect of free agency. Nonetheless, it is to the concern with autonomy that Locke's notion of freedom of action speaks.

In chapter 2, I argued that, in the second and later editions of the *Essay*, a mental state does not count as a choice unless it is an exertion of power conceived of in a particular way: conceived of *as* an exertion of power. I suggested that Locke's addition of reflexive awareness in his account of choice might be related to his view of personal identity; I suggested that this connection points to an account of the special kind of attributability that attends voluntary action, and I promised to return to this connection and analyze more closely what it means. It is here that I am fulfilling that earlier promise.

Now, Locke's account of personal identity is remarkably radical, more radical, in fact, than it is usually given credit for being. After all, Locke vehemently rejects the most natural way to think about personal identity. What could be more natural than to say that persons are just highly complex substances and, therefore, personal identity is no different from substance identity. I am the same person who drank down that cup of espresso an hour ago for the very same reasons that the espresso cup on the table is the same one from which I drank: both myself now and the espresso cup now are substances that maintain temporal and spatial continuity with those earlier substances. But Locke's denial of the claim that personal identity is to be equated with the identity of substance is a remarkably strong attack on this very natural thought. And, in fact, as Locke is well aware, a quite general lesson can be drawn from his arguments against the same-substance theory of personal identity: Personal identity is not founded on any metaphysical token underlying all the different stages of a person's life. What makes me now and the person who gulped down the espresso the same person is not that both person-stages are connected to some common metaphysical structure, whether material or immaterial. Personal identity consists in something else.

But what could it consist in? Locke gives us an answer: The various stages of a person's life are unified—are parts of a single thing—by virtue of relations of, what Locke calls, "consciousness" between the various stages. Locke tells us far less about the nature of "consciousness" than we would like. But this much is clear: For Locke, two person-stages are stages of the same person just in case the later of them is or can become "conscious" of the experiences of the earlier. Further, to be "conscious" of a past action is to conceive of it as performed by oneself.

And, if I am right, for an appropriate mental act to be a volition, a choice, the agent must conceive of it as an exertion of one of her powers; she must conceive of it as arising, at least in part, from herself. It seems quite likely that the kind of awareness that an agent must have of a choice for it to count as a choice is very closely related to the kind of attitude that an agent must have toward a past action for it to have been performed by her. The capacities that are central to being a person over time are inextricably involved in the constitution of choice.

This connection is interesting in its own right, but what does it amount to, what is its philosophical upshot? One point to make is this: Since Locke takes the boundaries of the person *over* time to be determined in just the way that the boundaries of the person are determined *at* a particular time—both are determined by the boundaries of "consciousness"—it follows that under Locke's mature account of volition, only persons are capable of choice, are invested with a will, for the very capacities that make us persons must be exercised for a creature to make a choice at all. It follows that only persons can achieve freedom of action, for freedom of action is dependency of action on *choice*—not dependency of action on other mental states (desires, whims) that might serve to bring about action. But, more importantly, I think the connection between the account of volition and the account of personal identity is a powerful resource for launching a suggestive (but ultimately incomplete) response to a problem that all causal theories of agency face. What this illustrates, I believe, is that there are philosophically powerful resources to be found in connections between the will and personal identity that can be harnessed in support of causal theories of agency.

Causal theories of agency are theories that analyze various action concepts by appeal to the causal etiology of certain events and states. For instance, in causal theories of agency, an intentional action is a state or event caused in a particular way by particular elements of an agent's psyche, usually intentions or choices. Such views vary with respect to the psychic elements appealed to and in other ways, but they have this much in common: the difference between a standard event, a happening, and an action, a doing, such theories claim, is to be found in the causal history of occurrences of each sort; actions are just states or events caused in certain special ways. Causal theories of agency tend to be naturalistic: they draw only on states or events as causes and effects and they invoke nothing stranger than standard occurrent causation of the sort that all philosophers must live with. It follows that, on causal theories, the causes of an action by virtue of which it is an action are not, themselves, actions; causal theorists of agency build doings out of happenings and causal relations. In my view, Locke was a causal theorist.[1]

The problem that all causal theories face—or, rather, the obstacle that all such theories must overcome—might be called the Where's the Agent Problem. The problem arises from reflection on cases in the same family as Frankfurt's "unwilling addict" (Frankfurt 1988b): the unwilling addict's pursuit of that to which she is addicted is driven by a desire from which she is alienated, a desire that acts on her, that makes her its victim. Examples of this sort illustrate a general problem: If we say that, for instance, an intentional action is one that is caused by an agent's intention in some normal way—that is, without some form of deviant causation—then we are open to the following objection: Couldn't the agent have been passive in the production of such an action? Couldn't the agent have simply stood there passively as her intention acted *on her*, causing her finger to twitch, the trigger to pull? Or, to put the worry a slightly different way, why should we say that the agent is to be equated with her intention? Why should we say that *she* put the oomph behind the action just because her intention caused the action to occur? In general, no matter what the concept of agency we are trying to understand—whether it is action in general or intentional action, or autonomous action—if we analyze it as an event caused in some particular way by events and states of an agent, there is always room to ask for a justification for equating those particular events or states with the agent herself. There is always the possibility, it might seem, that the agent could have been the passive victim of such events, and it follows, or at least it seems to follow, that no causal theory can serve to capture the crucial aspect of agency, the sense in which agents are *active*—as opposed to passive—in the production of their actions. In fact, we might say, without securing the active participation of the agent herself, that we do not paint the agent as *acting*—properly speaking—at all.[2]

Interestingly, Locke himself was confronted with an early form of the Where's the Agent Problem. William King, a contemporary of Locke's, wrote a short commentary on the first edition of the *Essay* that was sent to Locke.[3] In it, King worries that under Locke's account of the nature of the will, the will is nothing but a "passive power," and, King concludes, this is unacceptable, for the will is clearly an active power; we are active in the production of our own choices; they do not come upon us from without; they are not "crammed down [our] throat[s]."[4] This way of putting the worry is not quite the same as the Where's the Agent Problem, but it is a short step from it. It could be that what King was really worried about was that under Locke's account of the will, we might be the victims of our own choices, and, hence, we might not be active in the production of the actions arising from our choices. It is quite possible—although I don't know of any direct evidence to suggest this—that Locke revised his account of the nature of volition precisely because of the worry that King raised. Through revising his account of volition, Locke very well may have been trying to respond to the Where's the Agent Problem in the form posed by King. But even if that was not Locke's intention in revising his account of volition, that account provides a tremendous resource, I believe, for making (albeit incomplete) progress on a solution to the Where's the Agent Problem.

The notion of activity is not, perhaps, as well understood as it should be. However, a very natural way to analyze the notion—if we are to maintain naturalistic commitments—appeals to internality. An object is active with respect to a particular event or state when something internal to the object causes the event or state. In fact, as discussed in chapter 2, Locke analyzes the distinction between the active and the passive in just this way. Locke thinks that all events and states are either passions or actions of the substances in which they inhere, and he defines passions as follows:

> [A] motion in [a] solid substance is, when rightly considered, but a passion, if it received it only from some external Agent. (II.XXI.72)

The thought is that when nothing about a particular substance contributes to the production of one of its states, or an event that occurs within it, the substance is merely passive with respect to the state or event. It follows that under such accounts, an agent is active in the production of a particular event E when a state or event internal to the agent is one of the causes of E. (Notice that on this approach, a state or event can be internal without the agent being active with respect to it, for its cause might not be internal. Thus, activity with respect to one state is not inherited from activity with respect to another; in the causal history of every action, we eventually find states and events with respect to which the agent is not active.) Views of this sort, however, are doing a lot of work with an unexplained notion, the notion of internality. The obstacle facing analyses of this sort is that there are many different ways of understanding the notion of internality corresponding to various ways of drawing boundaries. It is difficult enough to offer a viable account of the boundaries of ordinary, everyday, physical objects. But it seems quite daunting to try to determine the boundaries of an agent. Further, there may be boundaries to be drawn within agents, and so states or events could be internal to an agent in one sense and external in another, and these different senses of internality and externality would correspond to different notions of activity and passivity with respect to the effects of these states or events. For instance, we might think that the rational self is only part of the whole self, so while a state or event could be internal to the self, it might be external to the rational self. If this makes sense, then we would be active in one sense with respect to events arising from states that are not part of the rational self, but are nonetheless part of the self, and at the same time passive with respect to such states or events.

Still, despite the difficulties faced by an appeal to internality in analyzing what it is to be active, I believe that such an appeal is the right way to go. What we need to know is whether there is some state or event that simply must, by its very nature, be internal to agents in the sense that the advocate of the Where's the Agent Problem denies. The advocate of the Where's the Agent Problem claims that no matter what state of an agent we pick to be in the causal chain leading to a putative action (or intentional action, or autonomous action), the agent could be acted on by that state or event in something analogous to the way in which she is acted on by the beating of her heart or by an epileptic seizure. I am suggesting that this claim rests on a particular, as yet to be identified, conception of internality. The Where's the Agent Problem could be paraphrased like this: No matter what state or event you pick to play a crucial role in the causal chain, there is always the chance that that state or event is external to the agent, and, hence, we cannot capture the sense in which an agent is a participant in her own action (or her intentional action, or her autonomous action) simply by appealing to the presence of such a state or event in the causal chain. Strangely enough, the advocate of the Where's the Agent Problem is willing to concede that the state or event appealed to by the causal theorist is a state or event *of the agent*, so she is willing to concede that there is some sense in which the relevant state or event must be internal to the agent. She seems to be denying that it must be internal to the agent in the sense that matters. But what does the advocate of the Where's the Agent Problem want? What is the sense of internality that seems to her to be lacking, or at least potentially lacking, from any particular state or event that the causal theorist takes to be the crucial cause of action?

Advocates of the Where's the Agent Problem are often—although not always—satisfied by appeals to agent-causation. (Two notable examples are Reid 1788 and, much later, Chisholm 1997.) They would prefer to put the agent herself in the causal chain leading to action and bite the bullet, or talk around, the mysteries of agent-causation. Perhaps this fact about advocates of the Where's the Agent Problem can help us to understand what they want. Notice that those who appeal to agent-causation don't seem to feel the need for appeals to substance-causation when discussing, for instance, standard physical causal interactions. In certain contexts, it is perfectly natural to describe the sun as the agent, the wax the patient, when the wax melts in the sun. But agent causal theorists don't usually insist that this talk be accounted for by saying that the sun itself—and not the heat of the sun—is the cause of the melting of the wax. What this suggests is that from the point of view of the advocate of the Where's the Agent Problem, the sense in which substances like the sun are active is adequately captured by appeal to the causal role of properties that are possessed by those substances, but the sense in which agents are active is not adequately captured by appeal to the causal role of properties possessed by particular substances that happen to be agents. But what are agents if not substances? Well ... they're persons. Perhaps what the advocate of the Where's the Agent Problem wants is that some state or event that simply must be internal to the agent qua person is in the causal chain leading to action. Perhaps if such a state or event could be found, then we would have found a state or event that can be thought of as playing the role of the person herself in the production of the events that it causes. Perhaps if such a state or event could be found, we would have found the agent in the causal etiology of action, for we would have found a state or event that is essentially internal to the agent and we would have found, therefore, a sense in which agents are active in the production of the events arising from these essentially internal states.

As I've said already, I think that Locke's account of volition—and particularly the connection that I am drawing to his account of personal identity—can help us to make considerable progress in responding to the Where's the Agent Problem. Recall: As I'm reading him, in Locke's account of volition, a mental act does not count as a volition unless it is accompanied by a special kind of self-conscious awareness of the volition itself. If we take seriously the idea that "consciousness"—however that notion is to be cashed out—is constitutive of personal identity, then it follows that that of which we are conscious is simply internal to the person conscious of it. The boundaries of the person are mapped by the boundaries of what she is conscious of; that is all there is to the idea that the person has boundaries at all. Further, under Locke's account of volition, choices are not just accidentally but *essentially* internal to us as persons. Choices are not merely internal to some substance, some mind, they are also internal to some person; if a mental act is not internal to a person, then it does not count as a choice at all.[5] In short, if it is the possibility that a state or event might be external to the person that worries the advocate of the Where's the Agent Problem, then we have found a state or event that answers her concerns, for choices, in Locke's account, are not and cannot be external to the person; internality of the relevant sort is part of what it is to be a choice at all.

Is this a satisfactory answer to the Where's the Agent Problem? (My answer, in short: almost.) One difficulty for the answer to the Where's the Agent Problem that I am proposing seems to come from the fact that it is possible to be passive with respect to one's choices. We can watch our choices, as it were, carry out their dirty business—such is, perhaps, the experience of the addicted or the compulsively perverse. This possibility points to a dilemma: on the one hand, I claim that the essential internality of choices, in Locke's account, secures the kind of active participation by the agent with respect to the effects of choice that causal theories need. On the other hand, it seems that we might be passive with respect to our choices. There is an apparent tension between these claims. But the tension is only apparent. (I put aside, to be discussed below, the (false) claim that we cannot be active with respect to a particular effect if we are passive with respect to its cause.) There is, undoubtedly, a sense in which we can be the passive victims of our choices. But notice that there is another sense of "passivity" in which we cannot be. Compare a choice to an epileptic seizure and imagine that both happen to bring about the same bodily movements; in the one case, I choose to perform a particular modern dance step, in the other I have an epileptic seizure that causes my body to engage in just the same bodily movements. If we accept the Lockean account of choice, then there is an important difference between the choice and the epileptic seizure: the seizure is, potentially if not actually, a state of my body that is external to me qua person; that is, it is a state which is, or at least could be, one of which I am not "conscious," in Locke's special usage of the term. What follows is that being a victim of a seizure is no different, or at least might be no different, from being harnessed like a marionette; the sense in which I'm the passive victim of a seizure is, potentially at least, no different from the sense in which I am the passive victim of the weather. On the other hand, a choice acts on me, and must act on me, from within. A choice simply is and must be mine, for internality is an essential feature of choices. Events arising from choices, then, arise from within me in a very different way from that in which events arising from seizures arise from within me. We are connected to our choices in a way that cannot be meaningfully abdicated even when we are alienated from the sources of our choices; there is no similar sense in which we are connected to our seizures. Choices seduce, seizures assault.

This is, in fact, part of the tragedy of addiction, of compulsion: the addict or the compulsive cannot help but see her degradation as arising, in part at least, from herself; she has no one else to blame. The actions that follow from our choices arise out of ourselves and are expressive of ourselves. Such actions are not, perhaps, or at least not always, expressive of the best parts of ourselves or the parts that we most wish to be expressed—there are senses of "internal," that is, in which choices can be external to us—but choices are expressive nonetheless of who we are as persons, and it follows that there is a sense of activity in which we cannot help but be active in the production of actions arising out of choices.

Another objection comes from the following observation: we could construct a category of essentially, necessarily, internal states that are not choices. For instance, we can imagine a subset of all seizures that are accompanied by "consciousness"; call them "conscious seizures." A state of an agent is not a conscious seizure unless it is internal to the agent qua person, for if it is not accompanied by "consciousness," it is not a conscious seizure at all. And, it follows, if Locke's account of volition secures a special kind of activity with respect to events and states arising from choice, that a similar kind of activity is secured with respect to events and states that arise from and depend upon *conscious* seizures. In fact, I think that this is correct, as far as it goes: We are active in an important sense with respect to events and states that are dependent upon essentially internal states of ourselves, even when those essentially internal states belong to constructed categories like "conscious seizures." But this isn't a result that we should find worrisome. I explain:

A first point to make is that we needn't be active with respect to "conscious seizures" themselves in order to be active with respect to their effects any more than we need to be active with respect to choices themselves in order to be active with respect to their effects. The fact that an agent can be active with respect to one state and passive with respect to its cause is an artifact of the analysis of activity through appeal to the internality, rather than the activity, of causes. And this is a good thing, for we cannot possibly be active with respect to a seizure just by virtue of being conscious of it. Further, this is a virtue of the analysis of activity through appeal to internality. If activity with respect to its causes was required for activity with respect to an event, we could never be active and, at the same time, part of the natural causal flow.

In addition, notice that when we analyze a concept like "intentional action" from within a causal theory, only one of the facts about such actions that we try to account for in our analysis is that the agent is active in the production of such events, events that count as intentional actions. We are also interested, for instance, in the fact that intentional actions might be, or follow from, the conclusions of deliberative reasoning. Further features of intentional actions beyond the agent's activity with respect to them are not going to be captured, probably, by appeal to states like conscious seizures, but might be captured by appeal to choices. There are features of choices that distinguish choices from conscious seizures—in Locke's account, for instance, choices consist in the turning of one's attention toward the production of action; no seizure, not even a conscious seizure, shares this trait with choices. It is the features of choices that distinguish them from conscious seizures that must be appealed to in order to account for the other important aspects of action, aspects beyond that of the agent's active role in the production of action. All that follows from the similarity between conscious seizures and choices is that both can be appealed to equally to answer the Where's the Agent Problem; there are undoubtedly other features of action that cannot be accounted for by appeal to conscious seizures.

What the appeal to essentially internal states—whether conscious seizures or choices—does is to frustrate a strategy for the construction of putative counterexamples to causal theories, examples of the sort that motivate the Where's the Agent Problem. Such examples are of agents for whom the causally crucial psychic element is external and who, nonetheless, count as actors according to the particular causal theory being addressed. The will of the unwilling addict acts on her "from without," and this is why, it seems, that it is false to say that intentional or voluntary action is merely action that arises from one's will. However, if an external act of will is not an act of will at all, examples of this sort do not show what they aim to show; they are not counterexamples unless they are examples in which the psychic elements claimed to be crucial are indeed causing states appropriately, but without securing the agent's active participation with respect to them. But if in order to remove the activity of the agent we need to remove the internality of the choice, then we can only be imagining a case of passivity with respect to a particular state or event when we imagine that the state or event that caused it is no choice at all.

Nonetheless, there is a problem with the proposed solution to the Where's the Agent Problem that can be seen through further reflection on the category of "conscious seizures." What is the difference between an agent whose modern dance step comes about as a result of a conscious seizure and the very same agent from whom the relevant consciousness is "subtracted"? The answer is: almost nothing. That is, the awareness of her seizure—even if accounting for its special internality—plays no crucial causal role in the production of her behavior. She would engage in the same bodily movement even if she were not conscious of her state, so why should it matter that the state fails to belong to the category of "conscious seizures" were she not aware of it? Similarly, on Locke's account of volition, the consciousness of the mental state plays no crucial causal role in the production of behavior; it plays a role only in determining what category the mental state belongs to. While we are frustrated from constructing the kinds of examples that fuel the Where's the Agent Problem by Locke's account of volition, we appear to be frustrated in this pursuit for the wrong reasons. We want our choices not merely to be essentially internal to ourselves; we also want the fact of their internality to account for their causal role. We want to be incapable of constructing examples of agents who are passive with respect to the force of their choices *because* precisely that which accounts for a choice's internality also accounts for its causal force. To put the point in Locke's terms, we want our awareness of our volitions as expressions of our active power to *account* for the fact that they are such expressions. As far as I can see, nothing in Locke's account of volition, as it stands, provides for this. Remedying this deficiency requires deepening our understanding of the relation appealed to in Locke's central insight about the nature of the will: Acts of will are acts of will by virtue of the relation they bear to the very features of ourselves by virtue of which we are persons. In Locke's account, the relation is no more than accompaniment: merely accompanying an appropriate mental state with consciousness is enough to promote it to the status of volition. However, accompaniment doesn't seem to be enough if we are to draw on the connection between the will and personal identity to solve the Where's the Agent Problem.

Nonetheless, what I hope has become clear is that Locke's account of volition, through its connection to the kind of awareness that is constitutive of personal identity, provides a powerful tool for answering the Where's the Agent Problem, even if more work needs to be done to deepen our understanding of the precise relation between volition and "consciousness." Despite its failings, the fundamental answer to the Where's the Agent Problem suggested by Locke's account is probably correct. Where's the agent? The agent is where choices are, because where there is choice, there is the kind of self-conscious awareness that defines the boundaries of the person.

Locke does not, as far as I know, explicitly connect his account of the nature of volition to the worry raised by King, the worry that in Locke's first edition account, the will is nothing but a passive power. Nor does Locke explicitly offer the response to the Where's the Agent Problem that I have been discussing. But there is reason to believe that Locke would have been happy to adopt such a response, for he does seem to employ a closely related argument. The Where's the Agent Problem can be described as posing a task: to paraphrase talk that sounds agent- or substance-causal into talk that draws only on standard occurrent causation. We are trying to understand how *I* could be the cause of my action; we are trying to understand how it is that it is *me* who deliberates, *me* who chooses, *me* who acts on my choices. But, from within a naturalistic causal theory of agency, we want to be able to say all of these things without relying explicitly or implicitly on agent- or substance-causation. What has been proposed so far is a suggestive, yet flawed, way of paraphrasing such talk through reliance on Locke's account of volition and its connection to his views of personal identity. While Locke does not explicitly follow the line of thought I have offered on his behalf, he does offer a closely related line of thought. That is, he explicitly suggests that certain agent-causal talk is rightly paraphrased through appeal to a state of the agent that is essentially internal to her qua person.

Consider, first, the following text:

> To the Question, what is it determines the Will? The true and proper Answer is, The mind. For that which determines the general power of directing, to this or that particular direction, is nothing but the Agent it self Exercising the power it has, that particular way. If this Answer satisfies not, 'tis plain the meaning of the Question, *what determines the Will?* is this, What moves the mind, in every particular instance, to determine its general power of directing, to this or that particular Motion or Rest? And to this I answer, The motive, for continuing in the same State or Action, is only the present satisfaction in it; The motive to change, is always some *uneasiness*. (II.XXI.29)

While Locke is happy to say, in general, that the agent determines her volitions, he does not think this is a satisfactory thing to say, without explanation, in particular cases. In particular cases, "The agent determines her volition" is to be analyzed as "Uneasinesses determine her volition." That is, he thinks that a claim to the effect that an agent determines an event—a claim about dependency of an event on an agent—is to be analyzed as a claim about particular states or events of the agent determining the event. What is missing here is any story about why it is that uneasinesses are essentially internal to the agent, and such a story is necessary for offering the best justification of the analysis.

But Locke has available to him an explanation for the internality of uneasinesses: Recall that uneasinesses are pains (cf. II.XX.6 and II.XXI.31), and Locke has the following to say about pain and pleasure, happiness and misery:

> If the *Soul* doth *think in a sleeping Man*, without being conscious
> of it, I ask, whether, during such thinking, it has any Pleasure or
> Pain, or be capable of Happiness or Misery? I am sure the Man
> is not, no more than the Bed or Earth he lies on. For to be happy
> or miserable without being conscious of it, seems to me utterly
> inconsistent and impossible. (II.I.11)

Locke is here making a commonsense observation: It makes no
sense to talk of a person being in pain or having pleasure if that
person does not feel it. Pains and pleasures are rightly attributable to us only insofar as we actually experience them. It is of
note, for our purposes, that Locke speaks here of being "conscious" of pleasure or pain in describing the awareness of pain
or pleasure that he thinks essential to it. And, interestingly, the
remark appears within the earliest discussion of personal identity in the *Essay*, a short discussion that appeared initially in the
first edition (and was included, as well, in all the later editions),
an edition that did not include the personal identity chapter.

Locke's insistence that we are always "conscious" of our pains
and pleasures is intended to be a conceptual rather than an empirical point; the very idea of having a pain without feeling it
is "impossible" and "inconsistent." In this respect, pains and
pleasures are, for Locke, like choices: a modification of an agent
cannot possibly count as a pain or a pleasure unless the agent
is "conscious" of it.

This suggests a natural justification for Locke's move from
the claim that the agent "determines" her volitions—that her
volitions are dependent upon her—to the claim that uneasinesses do, the same explanation that I have pointed to for the
analogous move in response to the Where's the Agent Problem:
As uneasinesses are pains, and pains always involve "consciousness," and "consciousness" is constitutive of personal identity,
to say that an agent's volitions are caused by her uneasinesses
is to say that they are caused by a state that is essentially internal
to her qua person, for a state of an agent of which she is not
"conscious" cannot possibly count as a pain.

In short, then, Locke's account of volition can be used to
make an important step toward a response to the Where's the

Agent Problem, and there is reason to think that Locke would have been friendly to such a use, since he seems to try to account for the sense in which we are active in the production of our choices through appeal to the essential internality of pains to the person, an internality that pains have in common with choices. We are active in the production of our choices for just the same reasons that we are active with respect to conduct that depends upon our choices; the causal force of uneasiness and the causal force of choice is the causal force of the agent, the person.

So much, then, for the first perfection. What connection can be found between the second perfection—determination of choice by the good, or the power to bring about such determination—and Locke's view of personal identity?

Contemplation of (Temporally) Absent Pleasure and Pain

We almost always think of the problem of personal identity in a backward-looking manner. That is, we almost always think that the crucial question is what it is that unifies the train of our *past* actions and experiences with those of the present. But one's present self is not the last stage in a life that began years before, but merely the most recent stage in a life that continues into the future. Something like this thought is what various thinkers have tried to capture through accounts of personal identity that incorporate not just memory links between the present and the past, but also links of anticipation and intention between the present and the future. Locke's discussion of personal identity does take backward-looking "consciousness" as the paradigm case of the attitude through which the boundaries of the person are constituted. But he is also concerned with present, and even future, directed "consciousness":

> [E]very intelligent Being, sensible of Happiness or Misery, must grant, that there is something that is *himself*, that he is concerned for, and would have happy; that this *self* has existed in a continued

Duration more than one instant, and therefore 'tis possible may exist, as it has done, Months and Years to come, without any certain bounds to be set to its duration; and may be the same *self*, by the same consciousness, continued on for the future. (II.XX-VII.25)

In the chapter on personal identity, Locke tells us little about the differences or similarities between "consciousness" aimed at the future and "consciousness" aimed at the past; future-directed "consciousness" is not his central concern, and it is easy to see why: He is centrally concerned with punishment for past transgression, so the relevant mental attitude is most important when it is aimed toward the past. However, it could be that "consciousness" aimed at the future is important for rather different reasons than "consciousness" aimed at the past. In Locke's account, "consciousness" of past actions—particularly "consciousness" of past transgressions of natural law—is important because of its necessity for just divine punishment (cf. II.XXVII.22, II.XXVII.26), but what importance could "consciousness" of future states and events have?

The answer to this question, I believe, arises out of a connection between future-directed "consciousness" and the capacities that Locke takes human beings to possess when they have (what we mistakenly call) freedom of will. When Locke thinks about transgressions of natural law, he mostly has in mind cases in which agents give in to temptation. Such agents gain some short-term pleasure—the pleasures of gluttony, of sexual indulgence—and are compensated later with the pains of hell. In such cases, what the agent would need to be "conscious" of at the time of punishment is the past pleasure gained through giving in to temptation. The agent must attribute the past pleasure to herself "upon the same ground, and for the same reason, that [she] does the present" pain (II.XXVII.26). In cases of giving in to temptation, the agent must, at the time of punishment, have a particular power: the power to reproduce past pleasures in some form or another and experience them as though they were present.[6] Through such a power, she can come to attribute the past pleasure to herself—since pleasure is always accompanied with "consciousness"—and thereby see the fitness of her punishment to her crime.

Recall that the power to raise in ourselves temporally absent pleasures and pains is discussed in "Of Power." There Locke says:

> [T]he removing of the pains we feel, and are at present pressed with, being the getting out of misery, and consequently the first thing to be done in order to happiness, absent good, though thought on, confessed, and appearing to be good, not making any part of this unhappiness in its absence, is jostled out, to make way for the removal of those *uneasinesses* we feel, till due, and repeated Contemplation has brought it nearer to our Mind, given some relish of it, and raised in us some desire; which then beginning to make a part of our present *uneasiness*, stands upon fair terms with the rest, to be satisfied, and so according to its greatness, and pressure, comes in its turn to determine the *will*. (II.XXI.45)

What Locke here refers to as "Contemplation" and elsewhere as "deliberation" is a process the outcome of which is the raising in ourselves of uneasinesses, pains, appropriate to those that we can expect through the performance of some particular action. Through "Contemplation," we feel pain in the absence of future pleasures and fear in the anticipation of future pains, and thereby give those future pleasures and pains an influence in the present determination of our wills.

As I've argued in chapter 1, the power to "suspend" the effects of present uneasiness for the sake of deliberation and "Contemplation" is of importance to Locke, since through the exercise of this power we can come to correct our uneasinesses in such a way that our wills will be determined by the good. We can come, that is, to imitate God—who "cannot choose what is not good" (II.XXI.49)—by gaining the power to bring it about that our volitions are determined, as God's are, by the good. This is the second perfection possessed by a full-fledged free agent: determination of volition by the good. Just as we need to become aware (or have the power of becoming aware) of the pleasure of giving in to temptation, as though that pleasure were present if the past action is to be rightly attributed to us, we must be aware (or have the power to become aware) of future pleasures and pains if we are to be full-fledged free agents, if we are, that is, to have perfection in the determination of volition.

While there is nothing essential to the capacities for raising absent pleasure and pain for full-fledged free agency—for all we know it might be possible to arrange determination of volition by the good without such capacities—it is also the case that human agents are full-fledged free agents by virtue of the fact that they are persons, that they are invested with these capacities. Persons, Locke thinks, are full-fledged free agents, if they are, only because they are persons, only because they are invested with the capacities that make it possible for them to attain perfection in agency. And this is really no surprise, for, as I've said already, Locke's discussion of free agency is driven by a desire to map out the nature of ideal agency, agency-at-its-best. Consider, again, the following passage:

> Would any one be a Changeling, because he is less determined, by wise Considerations, than a wise Man? Is it worth the Name of *Freedom* to be at liberty to play the Fool and draw Shame and Misery upon a Man's self? If to break loose from the conduct of Reason, and to want that restraint of Examination and Judgment, which keeps us from chusing or doing the worse, be *Liberty*, true Liberty, mad Men and Fools are the only Freemen: But yet, I think, nobody would chuse to be mad for the sake of such *Liberty*, but he that is mad already. (II.XXI.50)

Locke's thought here is that determination of volition by the good (or the power to produce such determination) is part of an ideal of agency, and this is why it is part of full-fledged free agency. Full-fledged free agency is something worth having, worth striving for, and so it cannot consist in the possibility of having one's volitions determined by something unworthy of an ideal agent. The possession of free agency serves as a hierarchical marker: creatures that lack it are lower than those that possess it. Personhood, similarly, is a hierarchical marker; those that lack it are lower creatures. Insofar as persons are capable of embodying the ideal that is free agency, it would be no surprise if it were through the right use of the capacities through which we qualify as persons in the first place, the capacities that raise us above mere animals.

But, in fact, the connection between personhood and the ideal of agency to which I am pointing is explicit in the passage just quoted. The word "Changeling" has a variety of connotations: in one usage it is a twisted or ugly creature put by fairies in the place of a normal human child; in another, it is a human being so altered as to become a fool or a madman. Locke mentions changelings in his rhetorical question for a reason: In all its connotations, to become a changeling is to give up one's personhood, and thus, it is to give up one's ability to resonate with temporally absent value properties in an appropriate way. But Locke is clear that to become a changeling is to give up free agency. Why should this be so? Only because it is through the right exercise of precisely those capacities that make us persons—that make us *better* than changelings—that we are free agents at all.

Locke's God—as is typical in the Christian tradition—is a benevolent God. And God, being benevolent, has a benevolent plan for human beings: God has arranged things to lead us toward eternal happiness. The kind of happiness of which human beings are capable is much greater than that of which animals are capable, for human beings can earn rewards for their good acts. On the flip side, the kind of torment—extended or even *eternal* torment—that human beings can earn is also far greater than that which any animal could expect. Animals can neither be punished nor rewarded, so there are heights of happiness and depths of torture that will never be theirs. For Locke, God threatens us with torture, and invests us with the capacities for fearing it, in order to direct us toward eternal happiness. But if God is to make it possible for us to gain eternal happiness, he must give us the kinds of capacities that make us the appropriate objects of moral laws, laws specifying the punishments and rewards for particular acts. The capacities that he gives us so as to make us the appropriate objects of the law are the capacities that are constitutive of personhood—we cannot be either punished or rewarded unless we can become "conscious" of past acts. But if the laws are to apply to us, we must not just be persons, we must be free agents. What I've argued here is that, for Locke, God gives us both sets of capacities in one fell swoop, for the capacities that make us persons are just those that, when used rightly, make us free agents.

CONCLUSION

The connections, then, between Locke's account of free agency and his account of personal identity are dual. It is because the attitude that is constitutive of personal identity is also essential to choice that we are active in the production of what we do when what we do depends upon what we choose. While there may be senses in which our choices can be external to us—they may not be internal to the rational self or the moral self—they are, nonetheless, internal to us as persons, and this takes us one important step toward accounting for the fact that we are active with respect to the events and states that depend for their occurrence on our choices. We have freedom of action, if we have it, only because we are persons. But, as I've mentioned already, a free agent isn't just active in the production of her conduct; she does not merely escape being a victim of circumstance, she also escapes herself; she is not a slave to her own parochialisms and peculiarities. What has emerged here is that, for Locke at least, this too is founded on our capacities for personhood. It is because we are persons that we are able to integrate temporally separate parts of our lives into a coherent whole and thereby come to respond to value in the world, value that is not instantiated in the here and now. When we respond appropriately, we begin to be the kinds of agents that we imagine ourselves capable of being; and it is then that we have liberty worth the name.

Notes

INTRODUCTION

1. All references to Locke's *Essay Concerning Human Understanding* are to Locke 1975. References to the "Epistle to the Reader" are given by page number; all others are given by book, chapter, and section number. The original date of publication of historically important texts is given in the bibliographical reference to the recent editions being used here.

2. Locke 1978, 4:625.

3. Those who hold a voluntaristic conception of value—who believe, that is, that what is valuable is a consequence of God's will rather than something that guides God's will—resist, thereby, the idea that an agent who is guided by love is really imitating the agency of God. After all, such an agent is not establishing, but rather following, the evaluative facts in her choices. Relevant here is Descartes's (a voluntarist, of course) discussion of the difference between our freedom and God's in the Sixth Replies. Descartes 1984, 2:291–92.

4. The canonical statement of Frankfurt's view is Frankfurt 1988b. Frankfurt has offered important revisions to this original view, but his position has not changed in ways that are important for my purposes.

5. One critic who brings this point up is Susan Wolf in the first chapter of Wolf 1990. Interestingly, Wolf's positive position bears interesting relationships to Locke's. In particular, both Wolf and Locke take freedom to consist, in part, in the dependency of choice on the good.

6. See my unpublished Stanford Ph.D. dissertation for an argument for this claim.

7. In the penultimate section of chapter 1, I discuss the question of the degree to which Locke's self-transcendence conception of freedom can be separated from his natural law theory. This question is crucial for understanding the degree to which Locke's view is of relevance to the contemporary free will debate, since few would want to accept Locke's natural law theory.

CHAPTER 1
A SECOND PERFECTION

1. I discuss power in much greater detail in the next chapter.

2. Hume 1975, 64–65; Malebranche 1992b, 448.

3. Vere Chappell has claimed that Locke adds to the Hobbesean picture by requiring both a power to do and a power to forbear as necessary for freedom, while Hobbes seemed to require only the power to do (Chappell 1994b, 103). As this quote suggests, however, there are some places at least in which Hobbes himself required both powers for freedom. It is also true, however, that Hobbes standardly seems to think that the power to act voluntarily is both necessary and sufficient for freedom. It is possible that the single power view is really Hobbes's settled position, and the passage quoted is misleading in this respect, but I leave the question for others to decide.

4. Notice that, for all that is described in the account of refraining contained in clause (2), an agent is rightly said to refrain from A when she voluntarily B's (where B is incompatible with A), even if, at the time that she B's, she gives no thought whatsoever to A. What this problematic fact illustrates is that a complete account of what it is to refrain from action would have to include certain epistemic conditions not mentioned here. This fact does not adversely affect any of the points that I wish to make about Locke's account of freedom of action.

5. I have just described Locke as a compatibilist. This claim is controversial. Peter Schouls (Schouls 1992) claims the opposite. John Colman, also, has claimed that Locke thinks that moral responsibility is not consistent with a mechanistic account of agency (Colman 1983, 207). Colman quotes the following passage, from Locke's discussion of innate moral principles, in support of his position:

[A] great part of Men are so far from finding any such innate Moral Principles in themselves, that by denying freedom to Mankind; and thereby making Men no other than bare Machins, they take away not only innate, but all Moral Rules whatsoever, and leave not a possibility to believe any such, to those who cannot conceive, how any thing can be capable of a Law, that is not a free Agent: And upon that ground, they must necessarily reject all Principles of Vertue, who cannot *put Morality and Mechanism together*; which are not very easy to be reconciled, or made consistent. (I.III.14)

What Locke says in this passage, however, is not that morality and mechanism cannot be put together but that some people are committed to the rejection of "all Principles of Vertue" because they fail to put morality and mechanism together. What Locke is concerned to argue here is that the fact that some people reject all moral principles on these grounds shows that moral principles cannot be innate, for if they were innate, then no one would think they had grounds for rejecting them. (It is not to my purpose whether or not this is a valid inference.) He is not agreeing with the grounds on which some people reject all moral principles. Rather, he is saying that in order to defend moral principles, we need to reconcile morality and mechanism, since appeal to the innateness of such principles is unacceptable. As Locke does not reject moral principles nor does he believe them to be innate, he must wish to reconcile morality and mechanism. Such reconciliation is one of the central tasks of compatibilism. So, in fact, this remark is actually a statement of Locke's commitment to compatibilism rather than a denial of the possibility of a successful compatibilism, as Colman claims.

6. Notice that the relationship between freedom of action and moral responsibility is not nearly so tight as the relationship between moral responsibility and voluntary action. Although there are many contemporary papers on the topic, two of the most important discussions are Frankfurt 1988a and Fischer 1994. Fischer and Frankfurt argue that the essential ingredient for moral responsibility is the agent's active participation in her conduct rather than the availability to her of alternative forms of conduct.

7. Hobbes 1648b, 43. Substantial selections from the debate between Hobbes and Bramhall appear in Chappell 1999.

8. I set aside the question here of the coherence and philosophical import of Bramhall's suggestion.

9. Some examples: In the account of secondary qualities, Locke is careful to tell us both what idea we usually express with color terms—the idea of the color as a real quality of objects—and what idea such terms should be used to express—the idea of a power in an object to produce certain ideas in us. Similarly, in the account of personal identity, Locke is careful to tell us what idea the term "person" stands for, and thinks that sufficient for having analyzed what it is to be a person at a time or over time.

10. Jolley 1999, 126, proposes a possible counterexample to Locke's claim. If I can become irritated by the fragility of a set of wine glasses (perhaps their fragility irritates me because of the exorbitant price of the needed packing materials), then doesn't the fragility of the wine glasses have the power to irritate me? If so, then a power can have a power, since fragility is a power of the wine glasses to break under certain conditions. Locke is not likely to be troubled by Jolley's example. It is not the fragility of the wine glasses that has the power to irritate me, but, rather, the wine glasses themselves by virtue of the fact that they have a certain molecular structure, a molecular structure that also accounts for their fragility.

11. This may seem like a forced reading of the passage. After all, Locke describes a group of people—those who are not content with freedom of action—and he seems to ridicule them as examples of people who are "willing to shift off from [themselves] . . . all thoughts of guilt." I seem to be claiming that he places himself in this group, and that doesn't seem to be Locke's intention in the passage. (This objection to my reading was brought to my attention by Vere Chappell.)

In defense of my suggestion—the suggestion that the passage counts as evidence that Locke saw freedom of action as insufficient for capturing all there is to full-fledged free agency—I should first concede that Locke does take a disparaging attitude toward those who are "willing to shift off from [themselves] . . . all thoughts of guilt," and he does believe that those people believe that freedom of action is not sufficient for full-fledged free agency. But, he also seems to assume in the passage that such people hold a particular view as to what more is needed for full-fledged free agency, a view that he is preparing to argue against. That is, the disparaging tone that Locke takes in the passage is toward a group of people whom he takes to hold two views: that there is an Elusive Something and that the Elusive Something is, genuinely, freedom of will. It is beyond question that he thinks little of the latter claim—he argues against it in the very next section of the chapter. In fact, as I hope to show by the end, he offers a view that is quite naturally taken as a view of the nature of the Elusive Something, so it is at least possible that he does not take a disparaging attitude toward the claim that there is an Elusive Something. It is, then, at least possible that the disparaging attitude that Locke evinces in the passage has its basis in the disparaging attitude that he holds toward those who believe that the Elusive Something is freedom of will, and not toward those who hold merely that there is an Elusive Something at all. In short, the passage is at least ambiguous in this regard, and the fact that Locke presents a positive view that plays the role of an account of the Elusive Something strongly suggests that it should be read as I am reading it.

12. See Chappell 1994 for a detailed discussion of Locke's argument for this claim.

13. We might argue that freedom of will consists in some other kind of freedom of action, freedom of action not with respect to volition but with respect to some other action. One way in which this might go is discussed below with regard to the interpretation that I call "The Elusive Something, Second Edition, First Try."

14. We might think that it is important which conception of the good guides our choice, despite the fact that we will be guided to the same action regardless. That is, we might think that it matters not just what you do but why you do it. If you do something because you think you'll get into heaven by doing it, then you are selfish, even if no matter how you looked at it you would still do the same thing. Locke, however, is insensitive to concerns about the relevance of reasons for action to moral evaluation, and I set aside the issues that such concerns raise.

15. Cf. II.XXI.39, first edition. The section is similar to II.XXI.61 of the later editions, but the differences indicate a change in view. In particular, in the first edition section, Locke describes mistaken judgment as representing something as good "to our choice," while in the later editions, he uses the phrase "to our desires." This is because in the first edition he takes the judgments themselves to be the appearances of good or evil that directly affect choice; in the later editions, he takes "uneasinesses"—sometimes referred to as "desires" or as the products of the faculty of desire—to be the appearances of good or evil, and sees judgments as influencing them.

16. I am putting aside discussion of agents who have accurate representations of the good accidentally. That is, I am putting aside discussion of agents who represent the good accurately, but the accuracy of whose representations cannot be explained merely by appeal to the evaluative facts.

17. Compare Susan Wolf's discussion of the person who answers "Carson City" when asked the question "What is the capital of Nevada?" See Wolf 1990, 72. Wolf suggests that sometimes, although not always, the best explanation for the fact that the person answered as she did is to appeal to the fact that Carson City is, in fact, the capital of Nevada. Similarly, the distinction being made here is between agents whose choices are rightly explained merely by citing the evaluative facts, and agents whose choices are best explained solely by citing their representations (or misrepresentations) of the evaluative facts.

18. I am assuming that causes must precede their effects in time. A could depend on B, even if B is a fact about the future, without thereby being caused by it. However, for those who are not bothered by the idea that causation could run backwards in time, there may be no difference between causation and dependency.

19. Locke 1978, 4:600–601.

20. Molyneux's criticism actually has another side to it, for Molyneux claims that in Locke's first edition account, sins proceed either from our understandings or else are against conscience. I discuss only the former objection in the main text; the reason that I ignore the latter objection is because it is based on a misunderstanding of Locke's first edition view: If we think of actions that are against conscience as being actions that discord with what the agent believes is right, then, under Locke's first edition account, it is not possible to act against one's conscience, for one's beliefs about what is right determine one's volitions. This is to say that under Locke's first edition account, weakness of will is impossible. For an interesting discussion of weakness of will in Locke's account, see Vailati 1990.

21. Molyneux's criticism could be taken as a criticism of the Platonic idea that to know the good is to do the good. If it is a consequence of the Platonic idea (as it seems to be) that a failure to do the good is a result of a failure of knowledge, then the adherent of the Platonic view is committed to the claim that sins indicate something faulty about our understandings, rather than our wills.

22. Locke 1978, 4:600.

23. Ibid., 4:625.

24. In the second and later editions, this same passage appeared (although in II.XXI.48 rather than II.XXI.30) with only one small change. In the first edition, Locke writes " '[T]is as much *a perfection, that the power of Preferring should be determined* . . ."; in the second and later editions, he makes one small addition when he writes, "*[T]is* as much *a perfection, that <u>desire or</u> the power of Preferring should be deter-*

mined . . . " (Emphasis added.) Locke adds the reference to desire because of his change in view as to the determinants of volition: the agent gains determination of volition by the good when her uneasinesses, also referred to on occasion as "desires," are determined by the good; her uneasinesses in their turn causally determine the will.

25. There are two points of ambiguity in this passage. First, it might appear that what Locke is discussing here is different from determination of volition by the good; he is discussing determination of volition by our "last" judgment of what is good. But, Locke thinks that there is correspondence between our considered judgment of what is good and what is, in fact, good. Further, it is clear from the context that he is talking of the same perfection that he has earlier described as determination of "the power of preferring" (that is, the will) by the good.

A second point of ambiguity: Under the interpretation for which I am arguing, Locke thinks that the "end of our Freedom," that is, the advantage that we gain by being free, is that, as a result, we are able to attain the greatest good for ourselves. The passage, however, says that the end of freedom is not that we might attain the good, but that we might attain the good *we choose.* I take Locke to be saying, however, that the end of freedom is that we might attain the good *by way of* choice. That is, the advantage that we have by being free is that we might get the good by means of choosing it.

26. As this passage hints, there is an interesting relationship in Locke's view between uneasinesses and desires. He says in one place (II.XXI.31) that uneasiness accompanies desire, in another that desire is a species of uneasiness (II.XXI.32). Locke is not terribly clear on the distinction between uneasiness and desire, nor does he seem to give desire (except insofar as it is no different from uneasiness) any crucial role in the determination of volition.

27. The interpretation offered here might seem to be in conflict with a passage quoted earlier:

> [W]ere [our volitions] determined by anything but the last result of our own Minds, judging of the good or evil of any action, we were not free, the very end of our Freedom being, that we might attain the good we chuse. (II.XXI.48)

This passage seems to intimate that volitions not only can be determined by judgments, but must be if we are to be fully free. What Locke must mean, however, if he is not directly contradicting his assertion that only uneasinesses causally determine the will, is that full-fledged freedom is what we have when our accurate judgments (equated with our "last" judgments—see the earlier footnote) guide the causal determination of the will by guiding the formation of appropriate uneasinesses.

28. In chapter 3, I draw some connections between the capacity to raise uneasinesses in oneself in accordance with future pleasures and pains and the capacities that Locke takes to be constitutive of personal identity.

29. Ayers 1991, 2:194.

30. To be completely thorough here, we also need to say that there are no circles, that is, no series of volitions V_i, $V_{(i+1)}$ . . . $V_{(i+n)}$ such that $V_i RV_{(i+1)} RV_{(i+2)}$ . . . $RV_{(i+n-1)} RV_{(i+n)} RV_i$.

31. What is suspension? In particular, how does it come about that an agent suspends the effect of her uneasinesses? Locke says little about the issue, but there is no reason to think that suspension shouldn't be treated just like any other voluntary action: suspension is brought about in accordance with a volition to suspend, a volition that is, itself, caused by uneasinesses. In fact, in a slightly different context, Locke makes it clear that suspension is voluntary action:

> [I]n Propositions, where . . . there are sufficient grounds, to suspect that there is either Fallacy in Words, or certain Proofs, as considerable, to be produced on the contrary side, there Assent, Suspense, or Dissent, are often voluntary Actions. (IX.XX.15)

(This passage is discussed in Losonsky 1996.) The kind of suspension that Locke is discussing here is suspension of assent to a proposition in the face of incomplete evidence, but there is little reason to think that he wouldn't treat suspension of the sort that leads to contemplation in precisely the same way. What this implies is that when we suspend, we do not prevent the efficacy of all of our "present" uneasinesses, but only those uneasinesses that are pushing us in one way or another with regard to a particular domain of action. In particular, we do not suspend the effect of the uneasinesses that are motivating us to suspend.

32. The "Third Try" differs from the "Second Try" in the following way: According to the "Second Try," an agent could possess the Elusive Something even if there is no correspondence between her volition and the good; so long as her volition corresponds to her judgment, even a mistaken judgment, then, according to the "Second Try," she has what she needs over and above freedom of action. According to

the "Third Try," such an agent (assuming she lacks freedom of action with respect to some action that would serve to arrange determination of her volition by the good) would lack the Elusive Something.

33. Some readers may be bothered by the disjunctive condition in this account of the Elusive Something. After all, it might be objected, if an agent's volitions are determined by the good, then she has the power to bring that result about, so the first half of the disjunction can be collapsed into the second. This, however, is not so, because it would be possible for an agent's volition to be determined by the good without her having the power to bring that result about. An agent who, for instance, is faced with an immediate choice—an action is "*once proposed to his Thoughts, as presently to be done*" (II.XXI.23)—might lack time to do anything to bring it about that her volition is determined by the good, and, nonetheless, her volition might be determined by the good because, say, she is appropriately disposed to appropriate uneasinesses, and so she doesn't need to *do* anything at all to arrange it that her volitions are determined by the good.

34. In fact, Locke's conception of what we mistakenly call freedom of will, his conception of the Elusive Something, is closely related to the conception of grace put forth by Augustine and developed in various early modern works such as Malebranche 1992a, which Locke is known to have read and been influenced by (cf. Vienne 1991).

35. One significant point about this passage is this: It is clear that there are times when deliberating does not help, but in fact hinders us from having our volitions determined by the good: if, to use a Lockean example, a rock comes flying at my head, I will waste valuable time if I sit down to survey my uneasinesses rather than just allowing them to bring about a volition on my part in favor of ducking. But notice that Locke is not a worshipper of deliberation. In the passage just quoted, he is careful to say that "the great inlet and exercise of all the *liberty* Men have ... lie[s] in this, That they can *suspend* their desires, and stop them from determining their *wills* to any action, till they have duly and fairly *examin'd* the good and evil of it, *as far forth as the weight of the thing requires*" (II.XXI.52, emphasis added). Locke's point is that we need deliberation only so far as it helps us to bring it about that our volitions are determined by the good, and no further.

36. Descartes 1991, 245.

37. One figure that is commonly overlooked is Jonathan Edwards. For a remarkably lucid discussion of moral necessity and the various shades of meaning of the term, see Edwards 1957, 156–62.

38. Leibniz 1969, 697. For an interesting discussion of the notion of moral necessity and its relation to freedom in Leibniz's philosophy, see Murray 1995. See also Yaffe 1999.

39. For a discussion of the importance of the imitation of God to Leibniz's view of freedom, see J. Davidson 1998.

40. Notice that if Locke held the view of the Elusive Something proposed in the "Second Try," there would be no meaningful distinction with respect to freedom between those who have mistaken judgments that accord with their volitions and those who have correct judgments. Thus, the advocate of the "Second Try" cannot offer a satisfying account of the purpose of Locke's remarks at II.XXI.69 discussed in the main text. Why should an agent with a corrupted palate have any diminished responsibility if the "Second Try" is correct?

41. Locke does not think that we always succeed in this endeavor. If, for instance, our "palates are corrupted," then imagining absent goods will not thereby raise appropriate uneasinesses in us. But Locke does think that we are almost always able to bring it about that our volitions are determined by the good.

42. We might wonder what kinds of forces could interfere with our freedom of action with respect to deliberation and, at the same time, bring it about that our volitions are not determined by the good. In fact, Locke gives some examples:

> [I]f any extreme disturbance (as sometimes it happens) possesses our whole Mind, as when the pain of the Rack, an impetuous *uneasiness*, as of Love, Anger, or any other violent Passion, running away with us, allows us not the liberty of thought, and we are not Masters enough of our own Minds to consider thoroughly and examine fairly; God, who knows our frailty, pities our weakness, and requires of us no more than we are able to do, and sees what was and what was not in our power, will judge as a kind and merciful Father. (II.XXI.53)

Certain uneasinesses, certain forms of pain, are such that when we are feeling them, we lose our freedom of action with respect to deliberation, and, at the same time, are led to wrong choices; such uneasinesses are "impetuous," they are not carefully considered, and there is therefore no reason to expect them to accord with the good. In such cases, we lack "liberty of thought"; we are not able to "examine fairly," to engage in deliberation, and we are at the same time caused to make a wrong choice.

43. Locke probably thinks that the relevant concepts from which the divine laws might be deduced are the concept of God and the concept of persons. This point seems to be expressed in II.XXVIII.18.

44. Locke 1963, 7:139.

45. There is a pressing question whether or not Locke's account of freedom of action is an adequate account of the kind and degree of self-expression in action that we crave even granting that it is not all that we crave from full-fledged free agency. I try to address this question in various ways in chapter 2 and in the first half of chapter 3.

CHAPTER 2
VOLITION AND VOLUNTARY ACTION

1. William Rowe and Myles Brand, for instance, both attribute a volitional theory of action to Locke. (Rowe 1991b, 1; Brand 1984, 9) In fact, both Rowe and Brand hold that, for Locke, the relationship that must hold between a volition and a modification for the modification to count as an action is a causal relation.

2. The term "passion" is used in a couple of different ways in the *Essay*; the definition in the text is the only usage that is relevant for our purposes here. The term is sometimes used as a generic term for any emotion or affective response, sometimes as a more general term for any mode of pleasure or pain that we endure. The latter of these usages probably bears some relationship to the notion of passion defined in the text—after all, what is it to "endure" a modification except to be nonactive (passive) with respect to it?

3. Locke uses the term "modification" in a rather broad sense. If a substance is changing, then the change is a modification of the substance. However, not all modifications are changes. A substance's state at a particular time is also a modification of the substance. Therefore, the state of a rock at rest is a modification of the rock. Similarly, the change from a state of not moving to a state of skipping across the water is also a modification of the rock.

4. Locke seems to leave open the possibility that proper actions are actions that are not caused by any modification at all, whether in the substance in which they inhere or occur, or in another substance. That is, Locke seems to leave open the possibility that proper actions are spontaneous or uncaused. If so, then the definition of proper action that I give here is not quite accurate. However, there is no reason to

believe that Locke thinks that spontaneous modifications are really possible, and none of the various modifications with which he is most concerned (such as volitions) are spontaneous (volitions are caused by uneasinesses). Therefore, even if he does leave open the possibility that some proper actions are uncaused, there is no reason to believe that he considers the set of uncaused proper actions to be nonempty.

5. Notice that there are some problems with this definition that are not easily overcome, at least not with any tolerable precision: Say, for instance, that I step on a rake that hits me in the head and causes a bruise. The bruise is a modification of me that was caused by a modification of the rake (its speed, position, etc.). But the modification of the rake was caused by a modification of me (the position of my foot, the speed of my foot, etc.). So, the bruise is caused, in part, by a modification of me (assuming some principle of the transitivity of causation). But the bruise is certainly the kind of thing that Locke wants to count as a passion of me rather than a proper action. Locke's account would need to be specified with greater precision in order to account for this example. The natural specification to make is this: A proper action is one whose *immediate* causes are at least partially internal to the substance in which it inheres. But the difficulty comes in specifying the notion of "immediate." This cannot mean mere temporal immediacy, since, after all, the bruise to my head is caused by the bursting of blood vessels in my head, which occurs after the occurrence of the rake's movement, and the bursting of blood vessels is internal to me. What we want to say, in Locke's defense, is that the bursting of blood vessels is "too close" to the bruise to make the bruise a proper action, while the stepping on the rake is "too far." But it is going to be extremely difficult—perhaps impossible—to specify precisely what the notion of causal distance (underlying the terms "too close" and "too far") consists in. In Locke's defense, albeit weakly, it seems to be true that we are able to effectively employ some notion of causal distance in understanding such cases, even if we cannot say clearly what that notion consists in.

6. Ayers 1991, 1:163 and 2:104.

7. A natural question to ask is this: Would a complete science of nature, by Locke's lights, eliminate the need to invoke powers? That is, is power talk eliminable through a full account of the qualities of objects by virtue of which events occur? This is, perhaps, another way of putting the question being tackled by the recent literature on Locke's views on substance and superaddition. See, for instance, Wilson 1979 and 1982, Ayers 1981, and McCann 1985 and 1986.

8. There is a strong parallel here to Locke's view regarding substance. A substratum is presupposed by our attributions of properties to objects, but the concept of a substratum is really a placeholder for we-know-not-what underlying structures that are responsible for us receiving the ideas that we receive from the objects. In fact, in places, Michael Ayers seems to think that Locke's views on power and substance are different ways of stating the same view. See Ayers 1975.

9. The distinction in attributability here is, in a sense, quantitative: more about a substance is expressed by a proper action than a passion. However, the difference in attributability that distinguishes genuine doings—occurrences of the sort that are crucially tied to moral responsibility—from mere happenings is not quantitative but qualitative. This is another way of making the point made already: The distinction between proper action and passion is not the distinction between doings and happenings.

10. We can imagine volitions being caused by other means: by God causing them directly, for instance, or through the influence of nefarious neurosurgeons. Such volitions are not proper actions and are therefore not expressive of an active power in us.

11. It is arguable that in the first of these two passages, Locke is also offering what we might call the Knowledge Condition on volition. That is, the first of the two passages seems to suggest that not only must we conceive of our volition in a particular way, but we must also know that we conceive of it in that way. The evidence for this comes from Locke's usage of the term "knowingly." Locke seems to be saying that in volition we do not just exert a dominion that we take ourselves to have over our bodies, but that we do so knowingly. But to knowingly take something to be the case seems to be both to take something to be the case and to know that you do take it to be the case. But if that is what Locke means, then he seems to think that satisfaction of the Conception Condition is not sufficient for the relevant act of the mind to count as a volition; we must also know that the Conception Condition is satisfied.

There is, however, a sizable amount of evidence against this interpretation. First of all, in the second of the two remarks quoted, the Conception Condition is explicitly mentioned, but Locke says nothing to intimate the Knowledge Condition. Further, as far as I can find, there is no corroborating evidence elsewhere to suggest that Locke held the Knowledge Condition. Finally, the Knowledge Condition is rather implausible, for it might require that we have to have the concept of volition in order to have volitions, and this seems plainly false.

12. Contemporary accounts of voluntary or intentional action have had little of substance to say about actions like sleepwalking. For a nice summary of recent work on intentional action, see Mele 1992. Also of interest, Williams 1994 and 1995.

13. Locke says only that volition involves turning one's attention toward the production of the action, not toward the *idea* of such production. This is just Locke being sloppy. In his official philosophy of mind, it makes no sense to turn our attention toward anything but ideas.

14. Locke 1978, 7:404.

15. There is only one passage that I know of in which Locke makes an effort to describe exertion explicitly. He says:

> [A]ll that [Lowde] says for *innate, imprinted, impressed Notions* . . . amounts at last only to this, That there are certain Propositions, which though the Soul, from the beginning, or when a Man is born, does not know; yet by *assistance from the outward Senses and the help of some previous Cultivation*, it may afterwards come certainly to know the truth of. . . . For I suppose by the *Soul's exerting* them, he means its beginning to know them, or else the Soul's *Exerting of Notions* will be to me a very unintelligible expression, and I think at best is a very unfit one in this case, it misleading Men's thoughts by an insinuation, as if these Notions were in the Mind before the *Soul exerts them*, i.e. before they are known; whereas truly before they are known, there is nothing of them in the mind, but a capacity to know them, when the *concurrence of those circumstances*, which this ingenious Author thinks necessary, *in order to the Soul's exerting them*, brings them into our Knowledge. (Footnote to II.XXVIII.11, Locke 1975, 355)

While the passage is discussing the exertion of "notions" rather than the exertion of power, it is striking that Locke says that there is no more to the exertion of a capacity to have a certain idea than the having of the idea when in certain circumstances. This remark is consistent with, although not direct evidence for, the account of exertion of power that I offer below in the main text.

16. We could offer an account of the nature of exertion of power by appeal to substance causation, rather than event causation. While Locke did not distinguish explicitly between event causation and substance causation, there are, as far as I know, no passages that cannot be given an event causal interpretation. (This is not to say that there are not also passages that can be given *both* a substance causal interpretation and an event causal interpretation.) Further, I believe (somewhat

controversially, I know) that an appeal to substance causation should be avoided for philosophical reasons, and hence the account of exertion that I offer here invokes only event causation.

17. I am drawing no distinction between "a volition to raise my arm" and "a volition in favor of my arm rising." I take both to mean a volition aimed at the production of a particular movement of my arm. That is, for our purposes, that which the agent aims at producing when having a volition is rarely itself a doing; it is rather a modification of a substance. That modification becomes a doing, as I am in the process of arguing, by virtue of its relationship to the volition. (I might anticipate that that which I choose will count as a doing by virtue of the fact that it will come about as a result of and in accordance with my choice to bring it about, but that does not mean that that which I choose is represented as a doing by my choice.)

18. Grice 1971.

19. Bratman 1987, 38.

20. John Colman makes the following remark about Locke's account of volition:

> In order properly to will, the agent must not only consider alternatives and settle his preference on one, he must at the time believe there to be some alternative open to him other than the action he chooses or prefers (even if it is only the alternative of not performing that action). (Colman 1983, 210)

There is, as far as I can tell, no solid textual evidence for either of the claims that Colman makes here, namely, (1) that for Locke, an agent has not willed unless she has first considered alternatives to the action on which she settles, or (2) that for Locke, an agent has not willed unless she believes that there were other actions available to her besides the one she willed. See the later footnote concerning Stephen Darwall for an objection to the claim that Locke holds (1). As for (2), Colman seems to be picking up on the self-conscious element in Locke's account of volition, but failing to see its import. To "take an action to be in my power" is not to believe that I had alternative possible actions available to me. Even if I believe that I will inevitably perform a particular action (engage in a particular modification), I may still believe that I have that action in my power, for I may believe both that the action will come about no matter what I do (as the man in the locked room might believe) and at the same time believe that it will come about if I will it and in accordance with my volition.

21. If Locke is offering the Knowledge Condition, which (as I've said) he probably is not, then we should add:

(4) (Knowledge Condition) S knows that (3) holds.

22. Notice that a mental act satisfying conditions (1) and (2) but failing to satisfy condition (3) might still be causally efficacious in the production of action. Further, such acts would be expressive of active powers in ourselves. These pseudo-volitions, however, are not true volitions; they are not the mental states that are expressive of the possession of a will. The active power that they express is a different, as yet unnamed, power. See the earlier remarks about sleepwalking and the volition-like states of animals.

23. Stephen Darwall has also noted that Locke made a large change in his account of volition between the first and second editions of the *Essay* (Darwall 1995, 159). Darwall does not try to extract a systematic account of Locke's view on volition from the revisions, but rather draws a series of conclusions regarding Locke's metaethical views about the source of the authority of morality. In particular, Darwall claims that the switch in Locke's view indicates that Locke came to see the will as a "faculty of self-conscious self-command" (Darwall 1995, 159). Darwall suggests that Locke made the changes that he made as a result of the influence of Ralph Cudworth's account of volition. According to Darwall, for Cudworth a mental state is a volition only when it is the final practical judgment reached in a self-comprehensive reflective act of deliberation (Darwall 1995, 136 and 141–44).

Darwall may be right that Locke altered his view after studying Cudworth's manuscripts, and he may be right that Locke came to see the structure of the will as playing a central role in the source of normativity. But it is wrong to suggest, as Darwall does, that for Locke, as for Cudworth, volitions are the last practical judgment of a self-comprehensive deliberative act; that is, it is wrong to suggest that under Locke's view of volition, it is necessary for an act of the mind to count as a volition that it be produced by such a deliberative act. Locke certainly thinks that the ability to engage in some kind of self-comprehensive deliberative act is crucial for freedom, but he is quite clear that there are lots of circumstances in which we do not engage in such deliberation and yet still have volitions (cf. II.XXI.9, II.XXI.23, II.XXI.24, II.XXI.50). Hence, his concept of volition cannot be quite the same as Cudworth's, even if it was influenced by Cudworth's manuscripts.

24. Lowe 1986, 150. Lowe formulates the definition of voluntary action in terms of actions and action-results. Since Locke never used this distinction, and all actions (in Locke's broad sense) are action-results, I formulate the definition without mention of action-results. "Modifications," in Locke's account, are the candidates for voluntariness. The definition tells us what conditions they must satisfy if they are to be successful candidates.

25. As it will turn out, no more than an appropriate volition is needed *causally* for a modification to count as a voluntary action; it's not as though a modification needs to be caused by something in addition to an appropriate volition if it is to count as a voluntary action. But more is needed *conceptually* for voluntary action than mere causation by volition; other, noncausal, conditions must be satisfied if a modification is to count as a voluntary action.

26. The paralyzed person may still be capable of engaging in mental actions in the same way as she could before she was paralyzed.

27. This point is elaborated below at the beginning of the subsection entitled "An Alternative Interpretation."

28. The reason that the conception is forced is that it suggests, implausibly, that almost no form of bodily damage can prevent the mechanism connecting volitions with bodily movements from being "in place." All that bodily damage can do on this model is to limit the functionality of the mechanism.

29. There is a claim in the passage of the causal sufficiency of volition for voluntary actions, but this doesn't imply that causation by volition is logically sufficient for voluntary action.

30. Important discussions of cases of deviant causation of action by intention or volition appear in D. Davidson 1980, 79 and 87.

31. For instance, imagine a baby who lacks the ability to scratch her nose. She might have a volition that her nose be scratched, and, following that volition, her father might serendipitously scratch her nose (maybe even using her own hand to do it), even though her volition did not cause him to do so. Did she, then, scratch her nose voluntarily? It doesn't seem so, yet she did have a volition to scratch her nose.

32. Lowe rejects an appeal to this tripartite distinction in another context.

33. There is one more piece of squirming to be done here on behalf of the Second Interpretation. It is possible that Locke was employing a tripartite distinction between the voluntary, involuntary, and nonvoluntary, but he uses the term "involuntary" to refer to the nonvoluntary.

Hence, under the Second Interpretation, the involuntary (as Locke should use the term, but doesn't) are all those modifications that are preceded by volitions that do not cause them, while the nonvoluntary are all those modifications that are not even preceded by volitions. This analysis of nonvoluntary seems to better serve the philosophical purposes for which a tripartite distinction is useful; the modifications of sticks and stones, for instance, which are nonvoluntary, are not preceded by volitions. However, under this analysis of nonvoluntary action, muscle spasms, heartbeats, and the like count as nonvoluntary rather than involuntary—an equally unsatisfactory result.

34. Locke offered his definition of voluntary action in the first edition in II.XXI.6 rather than II.XXI.5, where it appears in the second and later editions.

35. It is this line of thought that motivates the earlier suggestion that Locke's remark about paralysis is a slip on his part, a holdover from the first edition of the *Essay*.

36. Since the agent only conceives of volitions of the relevant sort as *usually* bring about the relevant actions, it would not be disconfirmed if the action did not occur. However, it would certainly not be confirmed, as it would be if the appropriate action was in fact brought about by the volition.

37. The following passage illustrates the point:

> [P]ersonality extends it *self* beyond present Existence to what is past, only by consciousness, whereby it becomes concerned and accountable; owns and imputes to it *self* past Actions, just upon the same ground and for the same reason as it does the present. (II.XXVII.26)

38. Perhaps we could countenance a difference in *degree* of attributability between voluntary actions and other proper actions by appealing to a connection between volition and the conditions on personal identity, independently of a retributivist conception of punishment. For intriguing efforts that can be taken to be aimed in this direction, see Bratman 1999, Frankfurt 1999a and 1999b, Korsgaard 1996, cf. 100.

Chapter 3
Free Agency and Personal Identity

1. On this point, incidentally, I follow Brand 1984, Lowe 1995, and Rowe 1991b, among others.

2. Various thinkers have presented and discussed versions of the Where's the Agent Problem. Notable examples are William King (discussed briefly below in the main text) and Reid 1788. In the contemporary philosophical literature, the problem has been posed and discussed by Hobart 1934, Chisholm 1997, and Velleman 1993, among others.

3. Locke 1978, 4:540.

4. Ibid.

5. Locke seems to take all mental states to be essentially conscious; in fact, this is arguably required for his argument against innate ideas in the first book of the *Essay*. However, the sense of "consciousness" in which all our ideas are conscious cannot be quite the sense of "consciousness" that is constitutive of personal identity. After all, Locke is quite clear that animals can have ideas, but animals are rarely persons (cf. II.XI.10).

6. It is not clear if "consciousness" of a past pleasure must be, itself, a pleasure. What seems important for Locke's purposes is that it be an affective state appropriate to the past pleasure. Perhaps the state appropriate to a past pleasure would be painful, a form of regret or remorse.

Bibliography

Adams, Robert M. 1994. *Leibniz: Determinist, Theist, Idealist.* New York: Oxford University Press.

Allison, Henry E. 1986. "Morality and Freedom in Kant's Reciprocity Thesis" *Philosophical Review* 45, no. 3:393–425.

Augustine. 1892. *The City of God.* Trans. M. Dods. London: Edinburgh House.

———. 1991. *The Confessions of Saint Augustine.* Trans. E. B. Pusey. New York: Quality Paperback Book Club.

Ayers, Michael. 1975. "The Ideas of Power and Substance in Locke's Philosophy" *Philosophical Quarterly* 25, no. 98:1–27.

———. 1981. "Mechanism, Superaddition, and the Proof of God's Existence in Locke's *Essay*" *Philosophical Review* 40, no. 2:210–51.

———. 1991. *Locke: Epistemology and Ontology.* 2 vols. London: Routledge.

Bennett, Jonathan. 1971. *Locke, Berkeley, Hume: Central Themes.* Oxford: Clarendon Press.

Berofsky, Bernard, ed. 1966. *Free Will and Determinism.* New York: Harper and Row.

Brand, Myles. 1984. *Intending and Acting: Toward a Naturalized Action Theory.* Cambridge: Massachusetts Institute of Technology Press.

Bratman, Michael. 1987. *Intention, Plans and Practical Reason.* Cambridge: Harvard University Press.

———. 1999. "Reflection, Planning, and Temporally Extended Agency." Unpublished manuscript.

Brown, Stuart, ed. 1991. *Nicolas Malebranche: His Philosophical Critics and Successors*. Holland: Van Gorcum Press.

Buss, Sarah. 1994. "Autonomy Reconsidered" *Midwest Studies in Philosophy* 19:95–121.

Butler, Joseph. 1975 (originally published 1736). "Of Personal Identity." In *Personal Identity*. Ed. John Perry. 99–106. Berkeley: University of California Press.

Chappell, Vere, ed. 1994. *The Cambridge Companion to Locke*. Cambridge: Cambridge University Press.

———. 1994. "Locke on the Freedom of the Will." In *Locke's Philosophy: Context and Content*. Ed. G.A.J. Rogers. 101–21. Oxford: Oxford University Press.

———. 1994. "Locke on the Intellectual Basis of Sin" *Journal of the History of Philosophy* 32, no. 2:197–207.

———. 1994. "Descartes' Compatibilism." In *Reason, Will and Sensation: Studies in Descartes' Metaphysics*. Ed. John Cottingham. 177–90. Oxford: Oxford University Press.

———. 1995. "Free Willing: Comments on Hoffman's 'Freedom and Strength of Will' " *Philosophical Studies* 77:273–81.

———, ed. 1999. *Hobbes and Bramhall on Liberty and Necessity*. Cambridge: Cambridge University Press.

Chisholm, Roderick. 1997. "Human Freedom and the Self." In *Free Will*. Ed. Derk Pereboom. Indianapolis: Hackett Publishing.

Clarke, Samuel. 1978 (originally published 1717). "Remarks Upon a Book, entitled, A Philosophical Inquiry Concerning Human Liberty." In *Samuel Clarke, the Works*. New York: Garland Publishing Company.

Collins, Anthony. 1990 (originally published 1717). *A Philosophical Enquiry Concerning Human Liberty*, Bristol: Thoemmes Antiquarian Books.

Colman, John. 1983. *John Locke's Moral Philosophy*. Edinburgh: Edinburgh University Press.

Cudworth, Ralph. 1996 (originally published 1731). *A Treatise Concerning True and Immutable Morality*. Ed. S. Hutton. Cambridge: Cambridge University Press.

———. 1996 (originally published 1838). *A Treatise of Freewill*. Ed. Sarah Hutton. Cambridge: Cambridge University Press.

Darwall, Stephen. 1995. *The British Moralists and the Internal "Ought."* Cambridge: Cambridge University Press.

Davidson, Donald. 1980. *Essays on Actions and Events*. Oxford: Oxford University Press.

Davidson, Jack. 1998. "Imitators of God: Leibniz on Human Freedom" *Journal of the History of Philosophy* 36, no. 3:387–411.

Descartes, Rene. 1984. *The Philosophical Writings of Descartes.* 2 vols. Ed. and trans. John Cottingham, Robert Stoothoff, and Dugald Murdoch. Cambridge: Cambridge University Press.

———. 1991. *The Philosophical Writings of Descartes, Volume III: The Correspondence.* Ed. and trans. John Cottingham, Robert Stoothoff, Dugald Murdoch, and Anthony Kenny. Cambridge: Cambridge University Press.

Edwards, Jonathan. 1957 (originally published 1754). "Freedom of the Will." In *The Works of Jonathan Edwards.* Vol. 1. Ed. Paul Ramsey. New Haven: Yale University Press.

Fischer, John. 1994. *The Metaphysics of Free Will.* Oxford: Blackwell.

Fischer, John and Ravizza, Mark, eds. 1993. *Perspectives on Moral Responsibility.* Ithaca: Cornell University Press.

Flew, Anthony. 1991. "Freedom and Human Nature" *Philosophy* 66:53–63.

Frankfurt, Harry. 1988. "Alternate Possibilities and Moral Responsibility." In *The Importance of What We Care About.* 1–10. Cambridge: Cambridge University Press.

———. 1988. "Freedom of the Will and the Concept of a Person." In *The Importance of What We Care About.* 11–25. Cambridge: Cambridge University Press.

———. 1999. "On the Necessity of Ideals." In *Necessity, Volition and Love.* Cambridge: Cambridge University Press.

———. 1999. "Autonomy, Necessity and Love." In *Necessity, Volition and Love.* Cambridge: Cambridge University Press.

Grice, H. P. 1971. "Intention and Uncertainty" *Proceedings of the British Academy* 57:263–79.

Hall, Roland, and Woolhouse, Roger, eds. 1983. *Eighty Years of Locke Scholarship.* Edinburgh: Edinburgh University Press.

Hobart, R. E. 1934. "Free Will as Involving Determination and Inconceivable without It" *Mind* 43:1–27.

Hobbes, Thomas. 1648. "Of Liberty and Necessity." In *The English Works of Thomas Hobbes.* Vol. 4. Aalen: Scientia.

———. 1648. "The Questions Concerning Liberty, Necessity and Chance, Clearly Stated and Debated Between Dr. Bramhall, Bishop of Derry, and Thomas Hobbes of Malmesbury." In *The English Works of Thomas Hobbes.* Vol. 5. Aalen: Scientia.

———. 1994 (originally published 1668). *Leviathan.* Indianapolis: Hackett Publishing.

Hoffman, Paul. 1995. "Freedom and Strength of Will: Descartes and Albritton" *Philosophical Studies* 77:241–60.

———. 1995. "Responses to Chappell and Watson" *Philosophical Studies* 77:283–92.

Hornsby, Jennifer. 1980. *Actions*. London: Routledge and Kegan Paul.

Hume, David. 1975. *Enquiries Concerning Human Understanding and Concerning the Principles of Morals*. Ed. P. H. Nidditch and L. A. Selby-Bigge. Oxford: Clarendon Press.

———. 1978. *A Treatise on Human Nature*. Ed. P. H. Nidditch and L. A. Selby-Bigge. Oxford: Clarendon Press.

Jolley, Nicholas. 1999. *Locke: His Philosophical Thought*. Oxford: Oxford University Press.

Kant, Immanuel. 1929 (originally published 1787). *Critique of Pure Reason*. Trans. Norman Kemp-Smith. New York: St. Martin's Press.

———. 1956 (originally published 1788). *Critique of Practical Reason*. Trans. Lewis White Beck. New York: Macmillan Publishing.

———. 1964 (originally published 1788). *Groundwork of the Metaphysics of Morals*, Trans. H. J. Paton. New York: Harper and Row.

King, William. 1732. *An Essay on the Origin of Evil*. Trans. Edmund Law. Printed by F. Stephens for W. Thurlbourn: London.

Korsgaard, Christine M. 1996. *The Sources of Normativity*. Cambridge: Cambridge University Press.

Leibniz, Gottfried Wilhelm. 1969. *Philosophical Papers and Letters*. Ed. and Trans. Leroy E. Loemker. Dordrecht: D. Reidel Publishing Company.

———. 1981 (originally published 1765). *New Essays on Human Understanding*. Ed. Peter Remnant and Jonathan Bennett. Cambridge: Cambridge University Press.

———. 1985 (originally published 1710). *Theodicy*. Trans. E. M. Huggard. La Salle: Open Court.

Locke, John. 1950 (originally published 1689). *A Letter Concerning Toleration*. New York: Macmillan Publishing.

———. 1960 (originally published 1690). *Two Treatises of Government*. Cambridge: Cambridge University Press.

———. 1963. *The Works of John Locke*. 10 vols. Aalen: Scientia.

———. 1969 (originally published 1693). *Some Thoughts Concerning Education*. Cambridge: Cambridge University Press.

———. 1975 (originally published 1690). *An Essay Concerning Human Understanding*. Ed. P. H. Nidditch. Oxford: Clarendon Press.

———. 1978. *The Correspondence of John Locke*. 9 vols. Ed. E. S. De Beer. Oxford: Clarendon Press.

———. 1990. *Drafts for the Essay Concerning Human Understanding and Other Philosophical Writings.* Ed. P. H. Nidditch and G.A.J. Rogers. Oxford: Clarendon Press.

———. 1990. *Questions Concerning the Law of Nature.* Ithaca: Cornell University Press.

Losonsky, Michael. 1996. "John Locke on Passion, Will and Belief" *British Journal of the History of Philosophy* 4, no. 2:267–83.

Lowe, E. J. 1986. "Necessity and the Will in Locke's Theory of Action" *History of Philosophy Quarterly* 3, no. 2:149–63.

———. 1995. *Locke on Human Understanding.* London: Routledge.

Mackie, John L. 1975. *Problems from Locke.* Oxford: Clarendon Press.

Malebranche, Nicolas. 1992. *Philosophical Selections.* Ed. Stephen Nadler. Indianapolis: Hackett Publishing.

———. 1992 (originally published 1680). *Treatise on Nature and Grace.* Trans. Patrick Riley. Oxford: Clarendon Press.

———. 1997 (originally published 1674–75). *The Search After Truth.* Ed. T. M. Lennon and P. J. Olscamp. Cambridge: Cambridge University Press.

Marshall, John. 1994. *John Locke: Resistance, Religion and Responsibility.* Cambridge: Cambridge University Press.

McCann, Edwin. 1985. "Lockean Mechanism." In *Philosophy, Its History and Historiography.* Ed. A. J. Holland. 209–31. Dordrecht: Reidel.

———. 1986. "Cartesian Selves and Lockean Substances" *Monist* 458–82.

Mele, Alfred. 1992. "Recent Work on Intentional Action" *American Philosophical Quarterly* 29, no. 3:199–217.

Murray, Michael J. 1995. "Leibniz on Divine Foreknowledge of Future Contingents and Human Freedom" *Philosophy and Phenomenological Research* 55, no. 1:75–108.

Passmore, J. A. 1951. *Ralph Cudworth.* Cambridge: Cambridge University Press.

Paton, H. J. 1958. *The Categorical Imperative.* London: Hutchinson and Company.

Paull, R. Cranston. 1992. "Leibniz and the Miracle of Freedom" *Nous* 26, no. 2:218–35.

Perry, John, ed. 1975. *Personal Identity.* Berkeley: University of California Press.

———. 1976. "The Importance of Being Identical." In *The Identity of Persons.* Ed. Amelie Rorty. 67–90. Berkeley: University of California Press.

Perry, John, ed. 1978. *A Dialogue on Personal Identity and Immortality.* Indianapolis: Hackett Publishing.

———. 1983. "Personal Identity and the Concept of a Person." In *Contemporary Philosophy: A New Survey.* 11–43. London: Martinus Nijhoff Publishers.

Polin, R. 1969. "John Locke's Conception of Freedom." In *John Locke: Problems and Perspectives.* Ed. John Yolton. 1–18. Cambridge: Cambridge University Press.

Raphael, D. D. 1991. *British Moralists 1650–1800.* Indianapolis: Hackett Publishing.

Reid, Thomas. 1788. *Essays on the Active Powers of Man.* Charlottesville: Lincoln-Rembrandt Publishing.

Rogers, G.A.J., ed. 1994. *Locke's Philosophy: Context and Content.* Oxford: Oxford University Press.

Rorty, Amelie, ed. 1976. *The Identity of Persons.* Berkeley: University of California Press.

Rowe, William. 1987. "Causality and Free Will in the Controversy Between Collins and Clarke" *Journal of the History of Philosophy* 25:51–67.

———. 1991. "Responsibility, Agent-Causation and Freedom: An Eighteenth Century View." In *Perspectives on Moral Responsibility.* Ed. John Fischer and Mark Ravizza. 263–87. Ithaca: Cornell University Press.

———. 1991. *Thomas Reid on Freedom and Morality.* Ithaca: Cornell University Press.

Schneewind, Jerome B. 1990. *Moral Philosophy from Montaigne to Kant.* 2 vols. Cambridge: Cambridge University Press.

———. 1998. *The Invention of Autonomy: A History of Modern Moral Philosophy.* Cambridge: Cambridge University Press.

Schouls, Peter. 1992. *Reasoned Freedom: John Locke and the Enlightenment.* Ithaca: Cornell University Press.

Sleigh, Robert. 1990. *Leibniz and Arnaud: A Commentary on Their Correspondence.* New Haven: Yale University Press.

———. 1996. "Leibniz's First Theodicy" *Philosophical Perspectives* 10 (Metaphysics):481–99.

Vailati, Ezio. 1990. "Leibniz on Locke on Weakness of Will" *Journal of the History of Philosophy* 28, no. 2:213–28.

Velleman, J. David. 1993. "What Happens When Someone Acts?" In *Perspectives on Moral Responsibility.* Ed. John Fischer and Mark Ravizza. 188–210. Ithaca: Cornell University Press.

Vienne, Jean M. 1991. "Malebranche and Locke: The Theory of Moral Choice, a Neglected Theme." In *Nicolas Malebranche: His Philosophical Critics and Successors*. Ed. Stuart Brown. 94–108. Holland: Van Gorcum Press.

Watson, Gary. 1995. "Freedom and Strength of Will in Hoffman and Albritton" *Philosophical Studies* 77:261–71.

Williams, Bernard. 1994. "The Actus Reus of Dr. Caligari" *University of Pennsylvania Law Review Symposium: Act and Crime* 142, no. 5:1661–73.

———. 1995. "Voluntary Acts and Responsible Agents." In *Making Sense of Humanity*. 22–34. Cambridge: Cambridge University Press.

Wilson, Margaret. 1979. "Superadded Properties: The Limits of Mechanism in Locke" *American Philosophical Quarterly* 16, no. 2:143–50.

———. 1982. "Superadded Properties: A Reply to M. R. Ayers" *Philosophical Review* 41, no. 2:247–52.

Wolf, Susan. 1990. *Freedom Within Reason*. Oxford: Oxford University Press.

Wolterstorff, Nicholas. 1996. *John Locke and the Ethics of Belief*. Cambridge: Cambridge University Press.

Yaffe, Gideon. 1995. "Freedom, Natural Necessity and the Categorical Imperative" *Kant-Studien* 86:446–58.

———. 1999. "Leibniz on Inclining Reasons and Moral Necessity." Unpublished manuscript.

Yolton, John, ed. 1969. *John Locke: Problems and Perspectives*. Cambridge: Cambridge University Press.

General Index

action: at a distance, 47; consciousness of, 114; different uses of term, 80; distinct from mere happenings, 75–77; God as pure, 6–7; involuntary, 104–7, 110, 157–58n.33; nonvoluntary, 106–7, 157–58n.33; overdetermination of, 18; performed 'with volition', 111; proper, 77–78, 84–89, 99, 103; refraining from, 15–16; volitional theory of, 78; voluntary, 87–88, 99–116, 121, 129–30, 157–58n.33, 158n.34; conditions on, 112; definition, 99, 109; wrong, 72

activity, 123, 128. *See also* action: God as pure

addiction, 4, 9–10, 19, 32, 121–2, 127–9

afterlife (eternal rewards and punishments), 33, 39, 66, 135, 138

agency, 3, 12, 24; active participation of agent in action, 122; boundaries of agent, 124; causal theories of, 121, 125, 129, 131; ideal, 6–8, 11, 72, 74, 137–38; Locke's metaphysics of, 77–88; in natural world, 87; perfection in, 137; problem of, 76

agent-causation. *See* causation: agent-

angels, 37, 55–56

anticipation, 134

appetite, 7

Aristotelianism, 34, 76, 82

attributability, 76–78, 85–88, 111–15, 153n.9, 158n.38; strong, 77

autonomy, 119. *See also* freedom as self-expression in action

awareness, 113, 119, 131

Ayers, M., 49, 51, 60–62, 82, 148n.29, 152n.6, 152n.7, 153n.8

belief, 40, 46–47

bliss, 58–60

Bramhall, Bishop, 19–20, 143n.7, 143n.8

Brand, M., 151n.1, 158n.1

Bratman, M., 95, 155n.19, 158n.38

causal chains, deviant, 104, 109

causal explanation, 82

causal interaction, 82

causal overdetermination, 106

causal theories of agency. *See* agency, causal theories of

Index Locorum